ACCELERATING CHANGE WITH

ORGANIZATIONAL

PROJECT MANAGEMENT

Keith,

Best of luck with
your project management
career ! Go Navy !!!

Walter

ACCELERATING CHANGE WITH
ORGANIZATIONAL
PROJECT MANAGEMENT

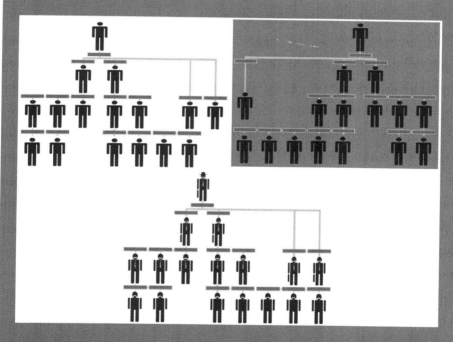

THE NEW PARADIGM FOR CHANGE

Dutch Holland PhD & Walter Viali PMP

To order additional copies of this book, contact:
Xlibris LLC
1-888-795-4274
www.Xlibris.com
Orders@Xlibris.com
134781

CONTENTS

    a.   The Sad State of Affairs
    b.   The New Way of Managing Businesses
    c.   A New Management Paradigm
    d.   An Emerging Discipline, Organizational Project Management (OPM)
    e.   A Valid Organizational Change Methodology: Engineering Organizational Change
    f.   The reason for this book
    g.   What you will be able to do after reading this book

PART ONE: THE NEW PARADIGM

    a.   What is the Problem with the New Reality?
    b.   The Old Paradigm: One Management System for Run-the-Business
    c.   What is the Run-the-Business Management System?
    d.   How does the Run-the-Business Management System handle change?
    e.   The New Paradigm: Two Management Systems for Run-the Business and Change-the-Business
    f.   What is the Change-the-Business Management System?
    g.   How does the Change-the-Business Management System handle Change?

PART TWO:
IMPLEMENTING THE NEW PARADIGM

PART THREE:
ACTION STEPS FOR IMPLEMENTING CHANGE AND OPM

CONCLUSION: THE NEW PARADIGM AT WORK

Dedication by Dutch Holland

This book is dedicated to the kids in my life: the little kids, Hope, Win, and Everett (E.J.), and the big kids, Eric, Wendy, and Bear. May they continue to flourish—and God Bless!

Dedication by Walter Viali

This book is dedicated to my wife Giulia, my parents, and to my brother Renzo, as well as to all those pioneers who have spent countless hours in their companies promoting OPM as a key discipline to achieving organizational effectiveness and competitive advantage."

A Note to the Reader

Each of us wants content "served up" in the way that best works for us. Deep down many of us wish "to get the answers in a few clever and memorable sound bites ("If the glove don't fit, then you must acquit . . . !" or "If they just don't get it, keep yelling until they regret it!") Sorry, but the explanation of the weighty and important concepts of successful organizational change takes more than sound bites. We have, however, written the book to be as accommodating as possible with three options for gaining value from our content. Good luck!

Option One: I just want the "meat," please!

If you are looking for a proven, easy-to-understand, easy-to-use model for successful organizational change, this is the right book. Just read Chapter One to get the idea that successful organizational change is all about breaking change into projects and then completing those projects . . . on target on time, and on budget. Then read Chapter Three to get the key idea that changing an organization is like a theatre company stopping an old play and transitioning to a new one . . . on target, on time, and on budget. And that's the meat? Yep, that's all there is to it . . . except for a few million details we will cover in the following chapters. (Not really, we will only cover a couple of dozen important action steps.)

Option Two: I just want to know about the people-side of change, please!

That seems to be a reasonable request, and we will try to help you out, although we will do so with some reluctance. As you read in Option One above, you should read Chapter One to get the "change projects ideas," Read Chapter Three to get the "theater company transitioning to a new play idea." If after reading those two chapters, you still want to restrict your learning to the people side of change, if you just want to know how to transition actors to a new play without worrying about all the trivial and irrelevant stuff like the script, the roles, the sets, props, and the contracts (since none of the aforementioned items need not in any way affect the actors in a play or workers in an organization), read Chapter Seven: Transitioning the performance management system. (If you want to read one more relevant chapter, even though such a chapter will cover stuff that's a little beyond the people side of change, read Chapter Eight which is all about using project management for guiding change.

Option Three: I want everything, big picture and all the details!!

If that is your goal, just read the book straight through. Take in all the logical steps for "what to do, what not to do, and how to do each step" for successful organizational change. Readers will get all the goodies they need to be able to transition their organization to Organizational Project Management and to nail the many change projects that must be completed for successful organizational change.

Preface

THE NEW PARADIGM FOR CHANGE USING ORGANIZATIONAL PROJECT MANAGEMENT

The present state of organizational change might charitably be called "a sad state of affairs." This sad state can be exemplified by three commonly-reported conditions:

- **Dismal Success Rates for Organizational Change**

  Success rates for organizational changes well below 50% continue to be quoted in the literature . . . after more than two decades of attempts to apply change management methods and expertise.

- **"Root Canal" Experiences**

  The literature is replete with stories and case studies about organizational changes that put organizations and their employees through what the Wall Street Journal calls "corporate root canal" experiences.

- **"Scared Stiff" Management**

  Many organizations contain "Frozen" managers who fail to implement needed changes because they are "scared stiff" of failure. Why would managers want to attach their names (and legacies) to change initiatives that have a high likelihood of failure to meet expectations and that put their fellow organization members through root canal experiences?

It is clear that the present ways of making organizational change happen are badly broken. And the books about change methodologies must be badly flawed, because the majority of lists of "change management actions" lead nowhere. In fact organizational change is so broken that the only to improve it is with a dramatically different way of managing today's businesses with their need for what seems like constant change.

The New Way of Managing Businesses

This book will describe three critical aspects of a new way of managing businesses that will enable organizations to survive and thrive in today's turbulent world. We will describe:

1. **A New Management Paradigm**

   The new paradigm for managing an organization requires two different Management Systems operating in parallel inside a single organization. The new paradigm that we call "Run-the-Business/ Change-the-Business" enables management and organization members to "do two things at once:"

   a. Run-the-Business to achieve this year's profit targets, and, at the same time . . .
   b. Change-the-Business to ensure the achievement of next year's profit targets.

2. **An Emerging Discipline, Organizational Project Management (OPM)**

   Organizational Project Management serves as the engine for the Change-the-Business Management System in the New Paradigm. This new discipline, OPM, a required core competence for today's organizations, includes the processes of:

   a. Visioning: Envisioning better futures for the organization,

b. Portfolio Management: Managing resources across a portfolio of initiatives needed to enable those better futures

c. Program Management: Managing programs or sets of projects to build the capabilities needed for a better future

d. Project Management: Managing individual change projects that apply bright minds to the creation of capabilities for better futures, and

e. Change Engineering: Engineering the newly-created capabilities into the day-to-day operations of the company.

3. A Valid Organizational Change Methodology: Engineering Organizational Change

Engineering Organizational Change (EOC)[1] is a proven and practical methodology for "organizational change . . . on target, on time, and on budget." Engineering is a critical function of the Change-the-Business Management System. EOC is built around the five key actions called for in the formula for organizational change:

a. Developing and communicating a vision: Step One in engineering change is to construct a "Vision of a better future" for the organization

b. Altering Processes: Designing and altering "work processes" to enable the vision of a better future

c. Altering facilities and technology: Altering or purchasing new "plant, equipment, and technology" to support altered work processes

d. Altering the performance system: providing "new assignments for organization members," new job descriptions, goals, training, evaluation and compensation

---

[1] *Change Is the Rule: Practical Action for Change . . . on Target, on Time and on Budget* by Winford E Dutch Holland, Dearborn Press, 2000

Project Management: Using disciplined "Project Management" to ensure that all the organization's key actions (above) are delivered . . . on target, on time, and on budget.

The reason for this book

Companies must change the way they do business from time to time in order to survive and thrive. Unfortunately most companies are not very good at making needed organizational changes on target on time and on budget.

Our goal in this book is to provide guidance and a suggested road map for managing a business using the new paradigm of Run-the-Business and Change-the-Business. The book will focus mostly on the Change-the-Business Management System that is powered by Organizational Project Management.

What the book is NOT about

This book is not about the technical details of Organizational Project Management or Run-the-Business/Change-the-Business.[2] We will not cover those subjects except at the summary level (we will leave the fine points of the disciplines inside RTB /CTB and OPM to another time). Implementing OPM requires significant organizational change, if it is to be done effectively. In this book the highly-technical mechanics of OPM are far less important than the organizational changes required for OPM to be implemented and make a difference in your organization.

---

[2] The details involved in using the dual Run-the-Business/Change-the-Business model can be found in its originally published form in the book *Change Is the Rule: Practical Action for Change . . . on Target, on Time and on Budget* by Winford E Dutch Holland, Dearborn Press, 2000, and the latest version of the model can be found in the book *How Managers Can Thrive in Waves of Change*, Dutch Holland PhD & Deborah Salvo EdD, Xlibris Press, 2012.

What you will be able to do after reading this book

- After reading this book, you will be able to appreciate and use the New Paradigm for managing your business. You will be able to describe and demonstrate Run-the-Business /Change-the-Business as a way of accelerating change in your organization, enabling more agility and faster response to needed change situations.

- After reading this book, you will be able to appreciate the need to have a discipline like OPM as a part of your organization's core competence . . . since changing your business is no longer the exception but the rule.

- You will be able to differentiate between situations that require the use of the Change-the-Business Management Systems rather than Run-the-Business Management Systems

- You will be able to understand and explain the Change-the-Business Management System and OPM as indispensable tools for today's organization.

- You will be able to lay out a roadmap to implement changes in your organization (changes like OPM), knowing what to do, when to do it, and in what order to get an organizational change up and running as a part of your organization's day-to-day operation.

- And finally, you will be able to see yourself as the leader of an initiative to implement both a change in your organization and to implement OPM in your own organization, knowing the actions steps as well as how to prevent organizational issues that will arise if not mitigated.

The organization of the book

Part One: The New Paradigm

In the first part of the book, we describe both the Old Paradigm and the New. The Old Paradigm is for managers to Run-the-Business as their primary focus and then to "improvise changes" as needed. The new Paradigm requires two parallel Management Systems for Run-the-Business and Change-the-Business.

Part Two: Implementing the New Paradigm

Implementation of the New Paradigm that includes Organizational Project Management requires a phased-approach for Awareness and Education, Pilot Projects, followed by Integration into the day-to-day work of the organization. Implementation requires "an organizational change" from operating with the Old Paradigm to operating with the New Paradigm.

Part Three: Action Steps for Implementing Change and OPM

The implementation of any change (like moving to the use of OPM) requires many action steps that must be executed in unison if the change is to be successful. The five chapters in Part Three of the book are laid out as a roadmap that can be followed to communicate a change to a new way of doing business, to alter work processes to enable the new way, to put in place tools and technology needed to support altered processes, and to alter the performance management system of changed assignments, training for the new way, evaluation and compensation.

Conclusion: The New Paradigm at Work

The wrap on the book is simple; the Old Paradigm for doing business must be replaced with the New Paradigm that uses two Management Systems in one organization. Failure to move to the New Paradigm of Run-the-Business/Change-the-Business will make today's requirement for organizations and managers impossible to meet.

> Today's organizations and managers must:
> - Run-the-Business well all the time, and
> - Change-the-Business well every time.

Part One:
The New Paradigm

Introduction

The New Paradigm for Managing the Business

The New Reality

A new reality has emerged for organizations and their leaders in today's turbulent and unforgiving business world. The new reality is the requirement for organizations to not only excel at running the business but also to be excellent at changing the way they run the business. Changing the way a company does business is necessary to take advantage of opportunities and/or to counter threats.

> **Change is no longer the exception for most organizations; change is now the rule.[3]**

With change as the rule, organizations will need to become very good at implementing changes. Change is no longer the exception in most organizations; change is now the rule. The need for most organizations can be stated as follows: "Since we are going to have to live under continuous marketplace and competitive change, we better get really good at change."

Many of today's organizations are good at Running-the-Business but not so good at Changing-the-Business, a condition that threatens every organization's performance and even their survival.

---

[3]   From **Change Is the Rule: Practical Actions for Change . . . On Target, On Time, and On Budget,** by Winford E. Dutch Holland, Chicago: Dearborn Press, 2000.

What is the Problem with the New Reality?

The problem is simple, even though the solution might be a bit more complicated. You see, companies will need to periodically change the way they run their businesses in order to survive (i.e., to stay up with the competition) or thrive (i.e., to exploit opportunities to move ahead of the competition).

Not only must organizations change the way they do business, they must make any such changes while the organization is working at full speed . . . to satisfy today's customers and to collect the dollars that will become a part of the company's profit. Figure I.1 makes the point that two important company actions need to happen simultaneously. In short, a company must Run-the-Business to make today's profit, while at the same time, they must Change-the-Business so that there will be a profit this time next year.

- **Run-the-Business to make today's profit**
- **Change-the-Business to ensure tomorrow's profit.**

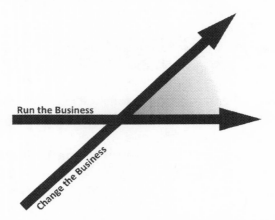

Figure I.1: The New Paradigm: Run the Business/Change the Business[4]

---

[4] The concept of two management systems in one organization . . . to **Run-the-Business and Change-the-Business** . . . was first published in the book **Change Is the Rule . . . Practical Actions for Change on Target, on Time, and on Budget**, by Winford E Dutch Holland, Dearborn Press, Chicago 2000

At this point the reader might say: "Ok that's all logical; so far so good. What's the problem?" The problem literally jumps out of Figure I.2 which shows the relative success rates of running businesses and changing businesses. The Run arrow shows a 99.97% success rate (a number we borrowed from Federal Express as their success rate in running their business of delivering packages).

The Change arrow carries a dramatically lower 30% success rate, a number that is often publicized in the literature. What? Yes, more than 70% of organizational change initiatives fail to meet management expectations!

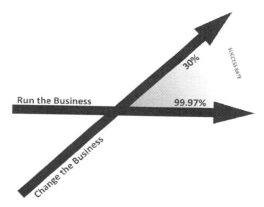

Figure I.2: Today's Success Rates for Run-the-Business and Change-the-Business

We know that Federal Express has a highly refined management system that makes their Run-the-Business numbers so sensational. But they are not alone. Almost every company that is surviving and thriving in today's rough-and-tumble world has a Run-the-Business Management System that works very well for them.

The successes companies are having with Run-the-Business Management Systems should be a lesson to us all. Management systems enable results. We believe that in many cases the high failure rate in organizational change is because companies do not have a management system to guide organizational changes.

The Old Paradigm: One Management System for Run-the-Business

The old paradigm for managing an organization is dominated by the Run-the-Business Management System. That's logical, of course. One might extend the logic to "one organization, one management system." Since the Run-the-Business Management System focuses on "products out" and "dollars in," it clearly must be the one system an organization needs.

What is the Run-the-Business Management System?

A Run-the-Business management system is the framework of processes and procedures as well as roles and accountabilities that enable the achievement of the organizational goal of profitable operation in the current year. The Run-the-Business Management System as we will use it in this book will be familiar to you. It is about marketing, sales, manufacturing, delivering of products and services and about getting paid on time. The Run-the-Business System is all about effectiveness, efficiency, and reduction of costs and process variation. In other words, run-the-business is about holding a steady course and being suspicious of any suggested change that might in any way threaten the smooth flow of products and services.

To meet annual business targets, the Run-the-Business Management System would be made up of organizational structure, defined work processes, policies and procedures, technology, equipment operating guidelines, job descriptions, training program, compensation systems, etc.

Most of today's companies are organized around "Running the Business" and spend the majority of their time in that Run-the-Business mode . . . until an organizational change is necessary. Until the last decade or two came along with its volatile business environment, organizations were relatively stable, and change initiatives were infrequent and could be handled on an *ad hoc* basis. "Muddling through" was the phrase that many managers used to mean . . . "we will get through this change somehow . . . and then we will get back to our real business of Running-the-Business!"

The structure and operation for most companies can be symbolized with a drawing such as the one in Figure I.3. Imagine the gray bar representing the way the company is organized to manage Run-the-Business (i.e., the Run-the-Business Management System). Imagine the Run-the-Business Management System being focused on annual business targets (e.g., for sales, customer satisfaction, safety, profit, cash flow, ROI, etc.).

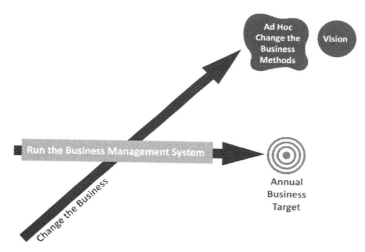

Figure I.3: Run the Business with Improvised, "ad hoc" Change Methods

- **How does the Run-the-Business Management System handle change?**

The obvious answer to the headline is "very poorly." The "change" picture for many of today's companies is very different from their Run-the-Business picture. Most companies, in fact, have little to no real organized effort or management system associated with organizational change at all. The absence of the gray bar for Change-the-Business in Figure I.3 is meant to symbolize the lack of an organizational structure and management system for Changing-the-Business (i.e., most companies literally have no Change-the-Business mechanisms whatsoever, with the possible exception of a capital budgeting process).

Run-the-Business Management Systems handle change by improvising around Run-the-Business. The odd-shaped blotch in Figure I.3 is to represent the activity usually associated with an attempted organizational change while in the Run-the-Business mode. Such change activity is almost always improvisational or "ad hoc," designed just for the occasion of the current change, and is filled with

- Change task forces and tiger teams
- Steering committees, panels, and councils,
- Internal change agents
- Change sponsors
- External change consultants
- Early adopters and late adopters
- Change advocates and Change Resistors
- Confused employees
- Befuddled middle managers and
- Frustrated C-Level players and, of course
- The inevitable small army of IT consultants from one of the billion dollar consulting/service firms.

And yes, there is also a CEO with the best of intentions for the company . . . working feverishly on his "Report to the Board" for their next meeting, dreading what he knows will be their first question, "Well, Mr. CEO, how is the organizational change coming along?"

Frequently lacking in such a "muddling through" change is a clear and detailed vision of how the organization should do business after the change, a valid change method, a change project charter, a master schedule and real personal consequences for those individuals who have been assigned to play change roles. While we have labeled the structure of the company that is associated with a change attempt as "ad hoc," meaning it was put together just for the current change, the best characterization of this change approach might be "improvising change while fighting fires in the day-to-day operation of the business."

No wonder change has such a low success rate . . . while inflicting so much pain on organization members. The Wall Street Journal just might win the prize of the century for labeling a big change, like implementing an ERP (e.g., SAP), as a "corporate root canal." And, for the most part, OPM implementation efforts have been no different. Project Management Offices (PMOs) have been put in place to get a better handle on the whole area of OPM, only to eventually fail and fall to the need to reduce overhead. Why does this happen, when we all recognize the importance of an orderly and predictable way of making change happen?

The New Paradigm: Two Management Systems for Run-the-Business and Change-the-Business

Today's new reality requires companies to Run-the-Business better than ever before. Customers press for higher quality products and lower prices while investors press for more returns. But the rapid advance of technology coupled with increasing competitive and regulatory pressures require companies to Change-the-Business far faster and better than ever before.

The new reality presents the following imperatives for today's companies and managers:

> **Organizations and their leaders must**
> - **Run-the-business well all the time . . . and**
> - **Change-the-business well every time.**

Running-the-Business well and Changing-the-Business well call for two complementary management systems, running in parallel. Organizations must run the business well all the time . . . and change the business well every time, and that won't happen by chance or by muddling through. Planned, organized, and collaborative Management Systems will be required.

What is the Change-the-Business Management System?

A Change-the-Business Management Systems is the framework of processes and procedures as well as roles and accountabilities that enable the achievement of the organizational goal of profitable operation in future years. Achievement of future profits comes about when a new and better vision and strategy have been developed and implemented into the day-to-day operation of the organization. A Management System is not a natural arrangement of activities but a contrivance of management; a contrivance that is only kept intact by the constant intention and attention of senior management.

A Change-the-Business Management System is particularly difficult to keep intact given that RTB does have almost all the organization's trump cards as well as a head lock on management attention and energy. For example, it is the rare manager who would walk away from a Run-the-Business opportunity to step into what most managers see as a change quagmire that is supposed to be focused on building capabilities for future profit. Run-the-Business also controls the "Red Phone" whose ring requires an immediate executive answer along with a dramatic shift in company and management priorities. With Run-the-Business holding all those cards and having all that attention and energy, it might be easy to see why company change initiatives might get short shrift.

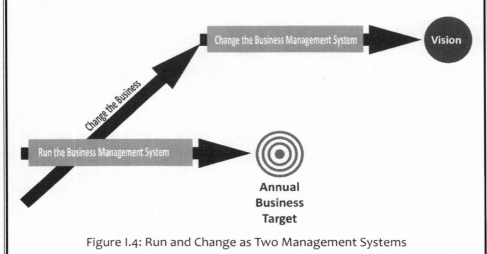

Figure I.4: Run and Change as Two Management Systems

How does the Change-the-Business Management System handle Change?

The Change-the-Business Management System guides change through continuous, orderly, and disciplined processes we call Organizational Project Management:

> o Designing a better future for the organization
> o Ensuring that resources are best applied to create the future
> o Organizing and leading initiatives to build capabilities that create the future
> o Applying the organization's best minds to design needed capabilities
> o Ensuring new capabilities are integrated into day-to-day operations

In response to the need for more agile, organized and successful change, management disciplines have formed and self-organized to begin to meet many of the challenges of Change-the-Business. These disciplines are at this time still in formative stages with lots more design and development work in front of them.[5] They have been coalescing as well into a system for change called Organizational Project Management (OPM), that include key functions for organizational change.

The remainder of this book will be dedicated to the exploration and explanation of these contents of functions of OPM.

Summarizing the Two Management Systems

Maybe this is the time to summarize our thinking about the two Management Systems (something that we also will do in more detail

---

[5] We know that some PMP readers of this book might be forming lynch mobs just now to punish the authors of such heresies. Let us explain. While Project Management and to some degree Portfolio and Program Management are "mature disciplines" having developed over literally decades in one kind of project-based organization (i.e., a project-based organization differs from a traditional administrative-oriented business), the development of the three functions has largely been in the context of Run-the-Business.

later in the book). Figure I.5 describes just some of the attributes of the two Management Systems that have emerged so far in our discussion of organizational change.

MANAGEMENT SYSTEM ATTRIBUTES	RUN-THE-BUSINESS MANAGEMENT SYSTEM	CHANGE-THE-BUSINESS MANAGEMENT SYSTEM
MANAGEMENT SYSTEM GOALS	• Hit Target Profitability this period	• Hit Target Profitability in future periods
SYSTEM IMPERATIVE	• Run-the-Business well all the time. 　o Maintain production, resist "changes," reduce variation, be risk averse	• Change-the-Business well every time. 　o Create vision, construct needed capabilities, implement capabilities
TIME FRAMES	• Continuous RTB with no time limits • Periodic changes to RTB	• Continuous CTB with no time limits • Designs periodic changes to Run-the-Business
SYSTEM LEADERSHIP	o CEO and COO	o CEO Executive Team
SYSTEM INTEGRATION	o Same Top Management Leadership team for both Management Systems	o Same Top Management Leadership team for both Management Systems

Figure I.5: Two Management Systems with Different Attributes

A cursory examination of the figure reveals distinct differences that will produce very different results. The examination also reveals the key to the simultaneous operations of both systems; namely the leadership of both systems comes from the same organization members, the executive team. More attributes will be revealed in the next chapter that is devoted to more information and detail about the Change-the-Business Management System.

Chapter One

Organizational Project Management

What is Organizational Project Management (OPM)?

Organizational Project Management is the engine for the Change-the-Business Management System. We have already defined the Change-the-Business Management Systems, but it is worth repeating here. A Change-the-Business Management System is the framework of processes and procedures as well as roles and accountabilities (i.e., OPM) that enable the achievement of the organizational goal of making changes to ensure profitable operation in future years.

The functions or work processes that we will describe below are the tools that senior managers can use to manage change in an organized and disciplined way. Before going on, we need to be clear that we are not saying that the creative thinking and innovation required of Change-the-Business can be "bounded, organized and disciplined." The functions in OPM organize portfolios, program and projects and manage them in a disciplined way while encouraging focus, innovation and creativity.

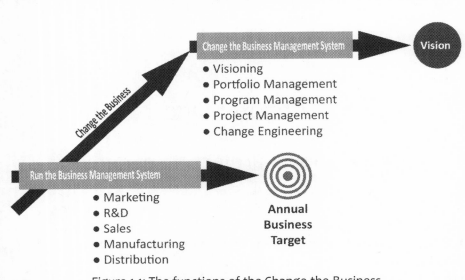

Figure 1.1: The functions of the Change-the-Business
Management System

What are the contents of OPM? That may take some explaining. The formal definition of OPM from *the Project Management Institute* (2013) is shown below:

> *"Organizational project management is the systematic management of projects, programs, and portfolios in alignment with the achievement of strategic goals [i.e., the vision]. The concept of organizational project management is based on the idea that there is a correlation between an organization's capabilities in project management, program management, and portfolio management, and the organization's effectiveness in implementing strategy [i.e., the vision]."*

The authors' experience, however, suggests that two more functions must be added to the three components already populating OPM: visioning and change engineering.

Figure 1.2: The Five Functions of Organizational Project Management

The first discipline to add is Visioning, the process of designing and describing valid and productive futures for an organization. Visioning as a function of OPM must be constantly "on" even though there may not always be a formal executive-led vision exercise going on. As a part of the visioning function, we include the determination of broad actions that organizations could/might/must take in order to put their vision into effect.

We also believe it is critical to add the function we call Change Engineering. We define Change Engineering as the discipline of putting project deliverables into day-to-day operation in the organization. For example, a project team might ready a software system for a company (i.e., complete a change project deliverable), but one critical task remains: preparing the organization to be ready for the software, or, as we say it, engineering the deliverable into the day-to-day operation of the organization. Change Engineering is the final step in implementing a company's vision/strategy, an implementation that must be completed before the company can begin to execute its strategy.[6] sponsorship

---

[6]   Because the operational focus and structure of a project-based organization differ from a traditional administrative-oriented business corporation, many business administrators--the middle managers--often view projects as costly and unnecessary activities that also threaten the organization's tried-and-true procedures and objectives. As a result, the administrative units cancel project initiatives; subsequently, project managers and business managers become adversaries. This book addresses how corporations can bridge the disparate professional approaches of business administrators and project managers through OPM.

and organization-wide education, a strategy that enables companies to transform their organizational structure while expanding their strategic focus and improving their competitive edge.

o   Visioning[7]—Designing a Better Future for the Organization

The idea of an organizational vision has gained popularity over the last few decades. We no longer talk about Long-Range Planning, and we speak softly about Strategic Planning.

For this book we will use our broad idea of visioning that includes (1) setting competitive and organizational strategies, (2) identifying the capabilities the organization will need to enact those strategies and (3) develop a vision statement of those strategies and capabilities at work. In short, the vision will be a picture of how the organization will look and act in the future as it uses its capabilities to compete to survive and thrive. In this book, we will not start with the mechanics of developing a vision but with deciding the Executive Team's intentions for competitive and organizational strategy.

1.   Developing Strategy[8]

Our first step in the overall visioning process is to develop strategy. Strategy brings focus to what a company strives to do in the market place (with customers and competitors) as well as the way the company will be organized and its resources used. An organization without a strategy is a rudderless ship.

---

[7]   The definitions of the words we will use in this part of the book are likely to be in sync for some readers and out of sync for others. The problem is that many of the words that will be used have multiple definitions . . . hopefully we can clarify as we go along.

[8]   Very Important! This book will be aligned with the thinking of Michael Porter, the guru of Strategy. Therefore, Strategy will be used as "competitive and market positioning" rather than an as an action plan to get a vision into play.

o **Competitive Strategy**

Competitive Strategy can be defined as the specific way in which the company intends to satisfy its customers while protecting itself from its competitors. According to Porter, we need to examine the following alternative strategies before making the choice for a company:

a. How can we make our products or services different so that customers will select us instead of our competitors?
b. How can we run our organization to produce high value goods and services at the lowest cost in our segment, allowing us to have more pricing flexibility in the market place?
c. How can we carve out a niche in a sector of the market and make our offerings so special that we become the "go to" destination for those customers?

o **Organizational Strategy**

Organizational Strategy can be defined as the way the company organizes and uses it resources to ensure the Competitive Strategy can be executed. Some of the ways a company can organize its resources are through centralization or decentralization, using contractors or full-time employees, etc.

2. **Designing Capabilities Needed to Enact the Strategy**

Once strategy is determined, top management must deduce the organizational capabilities needed to implement the strategy. An organizational capability is the capacity and the means to provide specific goods or services. The moving parts of a capability are work processes, tools and equipment, and competent human resources. Organizational capabilities added together and working in concert make up a complete business

The last major challenge for senior management in the Visioning step is to translate the executive-selected strategy for future prosperity into initiatives and/or projects in order to build and develop the organizational capabilities required to create that prosperous future. The development of organizational capabilities can only be led at the senior management level. We believe that the building of those capabilities is actually an engineering problem more than it is a people-changing problem. Putting new work processes, new tools and equipment, and revised performance management systems into place for a capability calls for very precise analysis and engineered solutions that are delivered with social finesse. And finally we are sure that competence in organizational mechanics is an absolute requirement for this last step of visioning.

3. **Developing the Detailed Vision**

    Once strategies and capabilities have been developed, attention can be turned to making those strategies and capabilities "real" for the organization. Reality starts with words and pictures that show the organization at a designated future time using capabilities to enact the selected strategies: competitive and organizational.

The next challenge for senior management is to craft a vision statement, a picture of how the organization will need to operate at some future time in order to use its strengths to capitalize on business opportunities. In a later section of this book we will talk more about the action steps needed to detail and communicate an organizational vision.

In this book, we are assuming that senior management has done its job and detailed a vision of the organization's future that, if reached, will be successful for the institution to either survive or thrive. We are also assuming that the central theme of the vision at this point has been decided, and reaching for that vision is now a requirement, not an option.

Our last assumption is that an Enterprise Program Management Office (PMO) has been opened. The purpose of the PMO will be to support the organization's visioning and planning process and help senior management develop the vision of the organization's future. The

PMO will assist management in the use of strategic planning methods, techniques, and tools to help develop and maintain the organization's strategy and ensure that the vision statement will be a living document and not end up on a shelf, never to be seen again as many do.

o Portfolio Management—Ensuring that Resources are Best Applied to Create the Future

Organizational strategies and the vision statement can only be implemented through change projects that build out necessary capabilities. Once executive management has identified a vision, a set of strategies and the capabilities needed to take the enterprise in the desired direction, potential projects supporting each strategy will be identified and grouped in a portfolio. Consequently, each portfolio will contain a mix of individual projects and projects grouped into programs, because of strong dependencies, that make it more efficient to manage them as interdependent efforts.

A simple definition of a portfolio is therefore a collection of programs and projects that support a specific business strategy aimed at achieving an organization's vision or a significant business objective.

> According to the 5th Edition of the Guide to the Project Management Body of Knowledge (PMBOK® Guide), from the Project Management Institute (PMI), "a portfolio refers to a collection of projects or programs and other work that are grouped together to facilitate effective management of that work to meet strategic business objectives. The projects or programs of the portfolio may not necessarily be interdependent or directly related.

For example, an energy firm that has the strategic objective of "maximizing the return on its investments" may put together a portfolio that includes a mix of projects in oil and gas, power, water, roads, rail, and airports. From this mix, the firm may choose to manage related projects as one program. All of the power projects may be grouped together as a power program. Similarly, all of the water projects may be grouped together as a water program.

Managing a portfolio has significant implications for an enterprise. As an organization's vision and strategies change, the portfolio will have to be revised to ensure continued alignment. This will require a "keeper" of this extremely important activity. Fortunately organizations are becoming more and more accustomed to the idea that this function can be performed by the Program Management Office (PMO) responsible for portfolio management, and consequently, for all the enterprise projects.

PMI's PMBOK® Guide states that "portfolio management refers to the centralized management of one or more portfolios to achieve strategic objectives. Portfolio management focuses on ensuring that projects and programs are reviewed to prioritize resource allocation, and that the management of the portfolio is consistent with and aligned to organizational strategies."

Given the increasing level of change that companies are experiencing in their business environment, managing portfolios of programs and projects is of paramount importance and not a one-off event. Maintaining alignment of portfolios and strategies can be a full-time job. The objective, of course, is to avoid spending valuable time and resources on programs and projects which are no longer relevant, if the strategy they were supporting is no longer valid or has drastically changed.

o Program Management—Organizing and Leading Initiatives to Create Capabilities

Program Management organizes and propels the Projects that construct concrete parts of the company's vision and strategy. These concrete parts are the capabilities that are necessary to enable the company's vision and strategy. Portfolios contain programs and projects. Programs are collections of closely related and interdependent projects. As such, these projects cannot be managed as unique efforts, as their interdependence with other projects will require a higher level of coordination across several of the projects components, i.e. risk management, procurement management, quality management, etc.

> According to PMI, a program is defined as "a group of related projects that is managed in a coordinated way to obtain benefits and control not available from managing them individually. Programs may include elements of related work outside the scope of the discrete projects in the program. A project may or may not be part of a program but a program will always have projects."

The figure below is designed to symbolize a PMO, providing direction for the change effort, providing alignment between projects, and giving velocity to the projects so that their deliverables mesh and are synchronized.

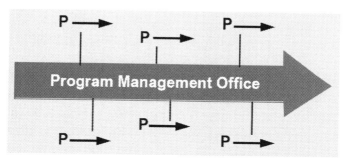

Figure 1.3: The Program Management Office (PMO)
with Six Projects (P)

A complex program can also contain sub-programs. There are many examples of programs, such as the Apollo Program and the Space Shuttle Program, which encompassed thousands of projects over their entire lifecycles. These projects were interconnected and typically managed as sub-programs, given the overall complexity of the goals to be met. This leads to the approach required to manage programs.

> PMI defines program management as "the application of knowledge, skills, tools, and techniques to a program in order to meet the program requirements and to obtain benefits and control not available by managing the component projects individually."

This form of "shared governance" among the many projects in a program allows a program manager to address resource constraints, as well as examining issues and scope change management requirements across the entire range of projects and not by examining individual projects on their own. This approach is key to achieving those economies of scale that a program can yield:

- Economies of scale that will come from volume purchasing of material and supplies to be consumed in a coordinated fashion by multiple projects,
- The analysis of probability and impact of risks that are common across the program's projects,
- The communication requirements and the quality standards identified for the entire program instead of individual projects. This will require superior planning and financial ability.

The role of the program manager is therefore of significant importance in the world of Organizational Project Management, as this individual will have to address the complexity of program and project management, along with the challenges of managing the organizational change that will come from the implementation of the products and services from the multiple program components.

The program manager will work closely with the project managers in charge of completing the various projects in the program, given the interdependence of these components. The program manager will also work closely with the portfolio manager to ensure continued alignment of the program components with the organization's vision. The program manager will also interface with the PMO, ultimately responsible for providing support to the teams working on the program components and for reporting status on the performance of these components and of the overall program.

o   Project Management—Applying the Organization's Best Minds to Design Needed Capabilities

Project Management is at the heart of the Change-the-Business Management System. Why? Because identified projects can best be completed by qualified team members who come from the organization and, sometimes, from the outside.

> Projects are the vehicles for bringing the company's best minds into the change effort. These best minds, subject matter experts, are key in building the organizational capabilities needed to implement company strategy. Selected team members can bring innovation and energy to any change initiative.

Ultimately, the portfolio and the program components, i.e. projects, will have to be initiated and managed in the most cost effective manner as possible.

> Project is defined by PMI as "a temporary endeavor undertaken to create a unique product, service, or result."

Too many projects have traditionally been completed well past their original schedules and well above their original cost estimates. During the past fifteen years, there has been a significant effort to qualify project managers through certification programs, such as PMI's Project

Management Professional (PMP®) certification, as well as provide improved methodologies for managing these efforts.

> PMI's PMBOK® Guide describes the process groups and the knowledge areas necessary to improve the way projects are managed, along with the most common tools and techniques used to get the job done as effectively and efficiently as possible. PMI defines project management as "the application of knowledge, skills, tools, and techniques for project activities to meet the project requirements."

In order to manage projects efficiently, the project team must clearly understand the scope of the effort at hand and build a comprehensive plan which includes the project schedule and several ancillary plans for managing not only the scope, cost and schedule of the project, but also its quality, communication, procurement, and human resource requirements. The team will also have to identify its project stakeholders and carefully manage their expectations until the end of the project (and often beyond). Last and certainly not least, the team will have to perform a thorough risk analysis on the individual activities and manage the identified project risks throughout the entire effort.

The PMO will play a key role on projects in supporting the project teams with experienced internal consultants and facilitators, who can assist the team in developing project deliverables, as well as time and cost estimates. The PMO will also provide risk analysis techniques and other standard and proven approaches for all teams to use and enhance the chances for success.

The rising cost of resources, both material and human, makes it imperative in these modern times to manage projects with the best methods, tools, and people available. All projects will also bring about varying degrees of change to the organization, which will have to be managed as part of the effort. Some of the best planned and managed projects have actually failed when completed in the absence of an effective change management process.

As projects and project management are now more than ever viewed as one of an enterprise's critical success factors, we can expect to see continued and increased emphasis on the qualifications required of those professionals involved in project work, along with ever more sophisticated processes and techniques to plan, execute, and control future projects, as well as to carry out effective organizational change.

o Change Engineering—Ensuring New Capabilities are Integrated into Day-to-Day Operations

Change **Engineering** works with the Run-the-Business Management System to ensure readiness to incorporate Change-the-Business project deliverables into day-to-day operations. While the intense focus has been on deliverables during most of Project Management, the focus now needs to turn to organizational change: changing the Run-the-Business operation so that the just-completed deliverables fit into place in daily operations. Vision and strategy are just wallpaper if the organization is not changed to create or enact the selected company direction.

> **The organizational change needed to put change deliverables in place in a "live" organization is not "a communication exercise" but a significant "engineering and construction challenge."**

The organizational change needed to put deliverables in place in a "live" organization is not "a communication exercise" but a significant "engineering and construction initiative." The effectiveness of both approaches to organizational change is known and quite different:

- **A communication-based approach,** regardless of how intensive that communication, will convince less than one third of organization members to comply with the new way of doing business, leaving two thirds of the workforce unchanged and either neutral or dead set against any change.

- **An engineering and construction approach** can be applied to the construction of an organizational capability. The engineering approach uses the entire change formula to put the new capability into play. This approach can get any needed organizational change in play . . . on target, on time and on budget, with 95% compliance at change-over time.

Change engineering, or the softer discipline of change management, is not a practical day-to-day part of project management. And in those companies that attempt to make Change Management a part of a technical project, failure is far more common than success.

The Moving Parts of the Change Formula

Successful organizational change, i.e., moving from one way of doing business to another, depends on the use of the engineering and construction change formula made up of the following "moving parts" shown in figure 1.4:

1. Communicating a new and exciting vision to the organization,
2. Creatively altering the organization's work processes,
3. Incorporating robust, powerful, and supportive Facilities, Equipment and technology (FET) into the organization
4. Re-structuring challenging roles for the organization's employees . . .
5. Disciplined Project Management[9] of all moving parts.

---

[9] "Wait," readers might say. "What is Project Management doing in this formula? Didn't we just complete Project Management to get here?" Yes, we just completed the OPM phase called Project Management during which an assigned deliverable was produced. The purpose of that project was to prepare a deliverable for the organization. The second appearance of Project Management signals a second project, this one focused on preparing the organization to use the deliverable.

Figure 1.4: The Moving Parts of the Change Formula

The moving parts of the organization are a system. Figure 1.5 below is designed to convey the idea that the engineering and construction formula is a systems solution to organizational change. Implementing just one part of the formula will not be accommodated by the other parts of the formula, and the attempted change will fail.

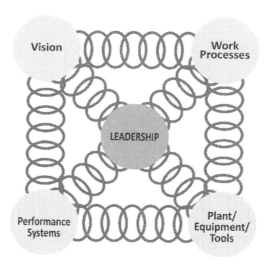

Figure 1.5: Mechanical Parts of an Organization as a System

Change engineering is a planned and disciplined effort to secure organization-wide compliance with the organizational change and the use of the deliverables . . . on target, on time, and on budget. Change engineering is not meant to be a "sales effort to get an entire organization on board." This last key idea is important to an understanding of change engineering and construction. Projects that have come to the change engineering stage of OPM have not arrived by accident or as the whim of some senior managers. Project management work has been serious, and deliverables have been constructed to fulfill a purpose as a part of an organizational change.

We have just covered the five functions of OPM: Visioning, Portfolio Management, Program Management, Project Management, and Change Engineering. Now it is time to describe how the five functions are linked.

OPM as a System; Continuous Operation and Continuous Improvement[10]

The five OPM functions work together. Change work flows from one OPM function to another rather than stiffly handing off to one another. Visioning feeds portfolio management, portfolio management feeds program management, etc. OPM is a top-down approach with plenty of room for participation and input from different parts of the organization.

As vision and strategy change, there is an avalanche effect. A portfolio must be continuously adjusted to realign with an organization's strategy. As the portfolio is realigned with strategy, programs and projects are impacted, with some programs and projects being reprioritized, some being eliminated (even if in progress), while others are added.

---

[10] A **system** is a set of interacting or interdependent components forming an integrated whole whose performance is more than the sum of its parts.

We then have to understand the overall impact on change engineering efforts. As we were preparing the organization for change due to the implementation of planned programs and projects, we now have to double back and understand how a new slate of programs and projects will impact our change engineering plans.

Looking at the five elements of OPM as a continuous lifecycle, we realize that this cycle never ends. Once it starts, it morphs into a permanent iteration of planning and re-planning with several implementation activities that may be impacted at any time by the world around us.

Market dynamics compel us to pay close attention to the five elements of OPM, as static portfolios not aligned with the organization's strategies can spell doom or cause significant setbacks. The PMO, the organizational unit tasked with keeping this machine well-oiled and constantly running is key, as the alignment and re-alignment of the five elements of OPM do not happen by chance.

A PMO should have enough talented people to help the organization's executives formulate their business strategies, based on organizational goals and market reality, and then understand how to prioritize and re-prioritize the other four elements of OPM, knowing that this cycle will never end. If an enterprise will not support OPM in this fashion, it could easily fail, but only after having wasted a tremendous amount of time and resources.

A PMO should also have enough talented people and backing to keep the OPM functions under continuous improvement. Ever cycle of OPM will result in lessons learned and then hopefully process alterations to ensure that the heart of the Change-the-Business Management System continue a healthy beat.

The Organization for OPM

Organizing for both the Run-the-Business Management System and the Change-the-Business Management System is a requirement, not an option. Four factors are critical for OPM organization:

- The organizational structure represented by the organization chart
- The Staffing of the Change-the-Business Management System
- The PMO staff organization and
- The organizational type.

Without clarity on the four factors, our observation is that there is a propensity to leave CTB work "blurred and confusing" . . . and at the same time, there seems to be a very strong tendency to try to use Run-the-Business methods, tools, and structure for Change-the-Business work. The following sections are designed to help clarify RTB/CTB organizations.

Organization Structure—Run-the-Business and Change-the Business . . . on the Same Chart

Organizational structure shows the patterns of relationships inside the organization. Organization charts, the visible expression of structure, are critical to see the division of work in the organization, the patterns and lines of authority and command as well as the relationship of divisions and/or departments. Organization members look to the organization chart to understand where they are in organizational space. Most organization charts represent the Run-the-Business Management System only, leaving employees in the dark about any change work they may have been assigned to do.

An organization chart that represents both the Run-the-Business Management System and the Change-the-Business Management System is shown in Figure 1.6. Note that the Change-the-Business System on the chart (the shaded area) containing OPM functions has equal visibility with the Run-the-Business system. Also note that there is one and only one hierarchy even though there are two management systems. Both the

Run-the-Business and the Change-the-Business structure report through the same executive to the CEO.

> **One organization, one hierarchy, one organization chart . . . and two Management Systems.**

Clearly shown on the chart is the direct connection of the Change side (shaded) of the organization to the CEO. While there is a CTB steering committee shown in the chart, note that it has an "advice and consent" role (represented by the dotted line) to the Change Program Manager(s). (More will be said about organization charts in the chapter covering Requirement Five for implementing change.)

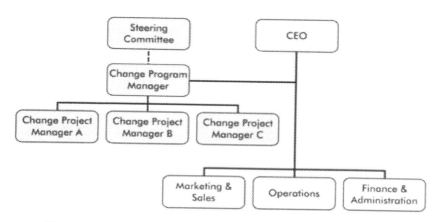

Figure 1.6: One organization chart shows both the RTB and CTB Management Systems

- **The Staffing of the Change-the-Business Management System**

While staffing for Run-the-Business operations is what we are accustomed to … with permanent employees in formal roles, the staffing for Change-the-Business is very different. With the exception of the Executive Team and the Program Management Office (that we will cover in the next section), all the other roles in Change-the-Business are played by specifically-selected personnel from all parts of the organization. Program Managers and Project Managers are selected by top management to temporarily serve for the duration of the Project/Program.[11] If there is not another assignment waiting in Change-the-Business operations, Program and Project Management personnel return to their full-time Run-the-Business jobs.

The Change-the-Business staffing at the executive level is permanent as it as for these same senior managers in their Run-the-Business assignments. In an organization operating with the New Paradigm that requires two Management Systems, the executives and senior managers must have the skills and competence to perform well in both Run-the-Business and Change-the-Business leadership roles. Gone are the days when a CEO could cherry pick her organization to identify a half dozen or so "good minds" to serve on a strategy development team. The harsh reality today is that if the Executive team is not the CEO's automatic first choice for her strategy development team, then she very clearly has the wrong folks in executive positions.

- **Program Management Office (the PMO)—Professional Staff to Support CTB**

The PMO for Change-the-Business is the permanently-assigned staff for the CTB Management System. The members of the PMO guide the Change-the-Business "machinery" and flow of work while the CEO and the Executive Team serve as the authorized leaders of any change initiatives undertaken by the organization.

While the organizational unit that contains or supports the OPM functions is generally called the "PMO," it functions very differently from the PMO we frequently see residing in the Projects-driven businesses or IT Departments of many companies.

---

[11]   Note that personnel in Program and Project Management positions in Change-the-Business are specifically assigned from their regular position in Run-the-Business. The "specific assignment" practice for Change-the-Business is very different from Program and Project Managers in organizations that are project-driven where Program and Project Managers may be permanently assigned to those positions.

Permanent staffing for the PMO should contain professionals with expertise in the five OPM functions. That needed expertise need not mean that there must be a manager or technical professional assigned solely to each of the five functions; some PMO members may be able to serve in more than one OPM function. In the New Paradigm, members of the corporate shop called Strategic Planning may be members of the PMO. In addition, in-house consulting staff may be housed in the PMO to serve as facilitators, OPM trainers and coaches.

While the PMO Manager reports to the CEO (or to another senior Executive Team member as designated by the CEO), the Manager is not in the chain of command for Change-the-Business. That chain of command must maintain the direct connection and "line of authority" between the CEO and the designated leaders of change initiatives who are typically line managers.

While the contents of the charter for an organization's PMO, or some might say, the "Enterprise PMO," may vary, some of the following attributes would be key in the staffing of the PMO. The PMO and its senior members should be:

1. Close to the CEO in both attention and visibility
2. Known for cleverness in the way the PMO can work inside an organization
3. Known to be very skilled in working with and influencing top-level management
4. Flexible, knowing more than one way to skin an organizational cat
5. Endowed with a high tolerance for ambiguity
6. Able to turn ambiguity into concretes (actions, ideas, etc.)
7. Known for their wisdom and experience in the business (i.e., they should have the "business in their bones")[12]

---

[12] "Having the business in their bones" is equivalent to saying that an organization member has been immersed in the critical details of the industry for a long period of time and is considered an expert.

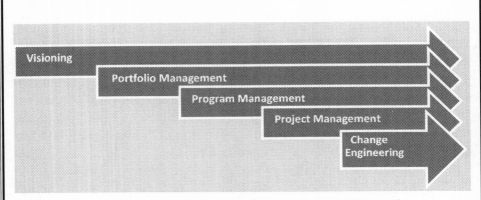

Figure 1.7: The Five Functions (and the flow of CTB work)
supported by the PMO

- **Two Different Organizational Types for Run and Change-the-Business Management Systems**

"An organization is an organization is an organization." That familiar statement is not true. Organizations come in different "types or forms," depending on the nature of the business environments in which they operate and on the intentions of management.

Two organization types have been identified that are both involved in the Run-the-Business/Change-the-Business way of managing: the mechanistic type organization and the organic type organization.

- **The Mechanistic type organization**

    The Mechanistic type of organization is tailor made for the Run-the-Business Management System. Mechanistic types of organization are based on formal structures, rules and procedures, and written communication. Such forms of organization are generally considered as inflexible, rigid, predictable, and standardized. Mechanistic organizations can pump out products today and tomorrow that are exactly like the products produced yesterday. Mechanistic organizations strive to reduce variation and to reduce risks from changes that might disrupt the flow of products.

- **The Organic type organization**

  The Organic type of organization is tailor made for the Change-the-Business Management System. Organic types of organization are more flexible, where organization members work together and coordinate tasks, communication flows in all directions; and fluidity of tasks is adaptable to changing conditions. Organic organizations strive to find business opportunities and design organizational capabilities that will allow exploitation of those opportunities.

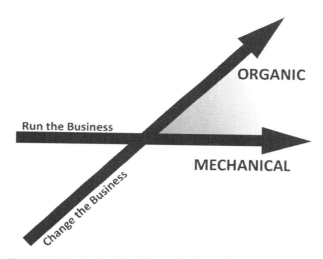

Figure 1.8: Organization Types for Run-the-Business and Change-the-Business Systems

The two different organization types and some of their operating details are explained in Figure 1.9. The two organizational types fit the Run-the-Business/Change-the-Business Management Systems to a "T."

Mechanistic[13] [Run-the-Business Management System]	Organic [Change-the-Business Management System]
Individual specialization: Employees work separately and specialize in one task	Joint Specialization: Employees work together and coordinate tasks
Simple integrating mechanisms: Hierarchy of authority well-defined	Complex integrating mechanisms: task forces and teams are primary integrating mechanisms
Centralization: Decision-making kept as high as possible. ○ Most communication is vertical.	Decentralization: Authority to control tasks is delegated ○ Most communication is lateral
Standardization: ○ Extensive use made of rules & Standard, and Operating Procedures	Mutual Adjustment: ○ Face-to-face contact for coordination. ○ Work processes tends to be unpredictable
Much written communication	Much verbal communication
Informal status in org based on size of empire	Informal status based on perceived brilliance
Organization is a network of positions, corresponding to tasks. Typically each person corresponds to one task	Organization is network of persons or teams. People work in different capacities simultaneously and over time

Figure 1.9: Attributes of Mechanistic and Organic
Organizational Forms Compared

We have previously written in the PMO section above that "This ain't your Mother's PMO!" Perhaps that statement also fits here as we show the two types of structures that need to work together in the same company.

---

[13] T. Burns and G.M. Stalker (1961).

A Case to Reinforce the Point

A huge multi-billion dollar dry-goods retailer was making major changes in the complicated systems they used to manage the tens of thousands of line items they sold. After much study and planning, a new way of doing business to be enabled by several state-of-the-art software applications was chosen and scheduled for an 18 month implementation. The COO charged with implementation oversaw the creation of a Change-the-Business team that included Program and Project management. Change roles were assigned and announced and the change process began to move toward the implementation target date through several Project teams.

In the middle of the project, the COO was promoted to another position, and the implementing organization change initiative was turned over to the experienced CIO. The new CIO was familiar with both Program and Project management from his position in a previous company and decided to beef up Change-the-Business by hiring a manager from a much larger company whose Run-the-Business work was largely project-driven. The new PMO Manager assessed the change situation in his new job as a retailer and concluded that everything was too "loose and flexible." With the CIO's permission, the new PMO Director implemented the tight, rule-bound PMO structure, policies and procedures that he had used well in his last place of employment.

Within a month, multiple Project Managers (who still had their regular Run-the-Business jobs) cornered the former COO to report that their progress was all but stopped. They reported that they were spending "all their time" in Program and Project meetings . . . and when they were not in meetings, they were filling out (or proof-reading) reports for the PMO! The former COO heard their concerns and initiated a conversation with the CIO, detailing the concerns of the Project Managers. "I can see their point," the ex-COO said, and the CIO nodded.

After the former COO and the CIO had talked, the CIO sat down with the PMO Director and talked about organization and management style. The CIO's request was "to reduce the level of bureaucracy" created by the PMO and to take a more supportive and flexible approach. The PMO Manager stated that with the amount of money the company had at stake in the change, it would be a betrayal of his professional responsibilities to do anything other than what he was doing. "In fact," he stated, "We still need to tighten up a lot more to ensure we stay in control of this change initiative."

The net result of the conflict was that both the CIO and the PMO Director were asked to find positions elsewhere. The company was forced to redirect resources from other parts of the organization to try to get the Change-the-Business organization back on track. They failed and the entire change effort was canceled in a few months.

As the originators of this idea say:

> Companies facing a dynamic and uncertain environment may have to develop or maintain an organic organizational structure [**Change-the-Business**], whereas companies operating in a more stable environment may benefit from developing or maintaining a mechanistic organizational structure [**Run-the-Business**].

> The reason for this is that organic structures can process and distribute information and knowledge faster within the organization, which thus results in an increased ability to respond or react to changes in the environment. [**The ideal structure for Change-the-Business**]

> However, mechanistic structures may act as an effective and efficient organizational structure for companies operating in a more stable and certain environment [**Run-the-Business**]. Companies operating in a stable environment may not need

to make decisions quickly. Likewise, many of the day-to-day decisions and operating procedures may be formalized and centralized, because there is no inherent need for constant change or innovation.[14]

Our cut on the comments above is shown below in Figure 1.10. The real issue is the need for a fit between the Management System and the type of organization that supports it. Our bottom line on this discussion is that using an organic type structure in Change-the-Business is a requirement, not an option . . . while using Run-the-Business thinking and mechanisms inside Change-the-Business is just plain deadly.

Management Systems	Mechanistic Type Organization	Organic Type Organization
Change-the-Business Management System	Poor Fit ... with a lack of flexibility, low innovation and creativity,	Good fit ... providing the flexibility and maneuvering needed for creativity
Run-the-Business Management System	Good fit ... providing the structure, rules, and procedures needed for product quality and reliability	Poor fit ... with a lack of standardization and stability in product systems resulting in poor quality of products

Figure 1.10: Fit of Management System and Organizational Type

---

[14] These paragraphs are based upon the work done by the theorists T. Burns and G.M. Stalker (1961).

The practical implications of the two types means that both kinds of organization structures will need to be operative in today's company at the same time. Another implication is that company employees who work part of their day in their Run-the-Business assignments and other parts of their day in their Change-the-Business assignments will need to be able to switch from one way of operating to another several times per week. While the need to switch may seem difficult to some, in practice the "switch gears" move goes smoothly.

- **Staying Focused on the Vision**

Focusing on the vision prevents "throwing the baby out with the bathwater." That idea has a connection here because, in the workings of an organizational change and in the machinations of OPM, a lot of bathwater is created, sometimes enough to lose sight of the intentions for organizational change.

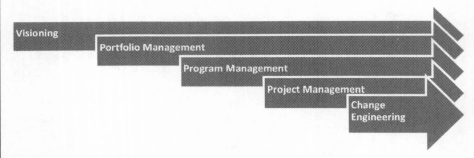

Figure 1.11: Visioning as the Thread of Continuity in OPM

In theater terms the central idea that must be supported and maintained through the production and performance of the play is called the "spine of the play" or the "thread" (running through Visioning in Figure 1.10). If we consider that an organizational change to a new way of doing business looks like "changing the play" for the organization, it is important to understand that the attempted change has a spine as well, a central idea that captures the essence of the change.

Some would say the spine of an organizational change is the "executive intent for the change." Others might say that the "competitive and organizational strategies" developed during visioning should be the thread because once decided in the visioning process, they become the foundation that should remain unchanged.

The point is that the PMO and the functions of OPM as described in this book must always be aligned with and subordinate to "executive intent" which hopefully is clear in the vision for the organization's new way of doing business.

While we would love to write more about OPM, we must remember the spine of this book. Our job is not to explain OPM in great detail but to take apart and put back together the implementation of OPM into a company that lacks a Change-the-Business Management System.

One Organization, One Hierarchy, One Population, Two Management Systems. Accelerating change to better compete in today's turbulent environment takes the complementary work of two management systems in one organization: Run-the-Business, Change-the-Business. The systems generally have different attributes and, in some cases, the same attributes. For example, the RTB system resists anything that interrupts production while the CTB system creates new capabilities to reach a new vision.

Both Management Systems use a hierarchy under an overall company hierarchy, but the hierarchies are of different organizational types: mechanistic and organic. Finally, both systems are ultimately led and coordinated by the CEO, the only organization member that has the authority to make critical organizational changes. More of the differences and similarities of the two management systems are shown in Figure 1.12.

We might say that we have described OPM just the way it needs to be, and now we will work to explain its implementation. However, it is not our concept of OPM that should be implemented. Each company must define its own version of OPM that would best suit its

Each company must define its own version of OPM that would best suit its situation.

situation. OPM in one company could begin at the project level and grow bottom-up towards Program Management and, eventually Portfolio Management and Visioning. In another company, we could witness an OPM top-down implementation from the very beginning. That is, the company could establish an Enterprise PMO to immediately lead the OPM implementation effort from Visioning through Change Engineering. At any rate, let the implementation discussion begin.

One Organization: Two Complementary Management Systems with Different Attributes

The new paradigm is One Organization: Two Management Systems. As we have said before, the two systems are different but complementary. Figure 1.12 below summarizes the attributes of the two Management Systems.

MANAGEMENT SYSTEM ATTRIBUTES	RUN-THE-BUSINESS MANAGEMENT SYSTEM	CHANGE-THE-BUSINESS MANAGEMENT SYSTEM
SYSTEM GOALS	• Hit Target Profitability this period	• Profitability in future periods

SYSTEM IMPERATIVE	• Run the Business well all the time.
	   ○ Maintain production, resist "changes," reduce variation, be risk averse
		• Change the Business well every time.
		   ○ Create vision, construct needed capabilities, implement

SYSTEMS FUNCTIONS	• Marketing • R&D • Sales • Manufacturing • Distribution	• Visioning • Portfolio Management • Program Management • Project Management • Change Engineering
MANAGEMENT FUNCTIONS	• Plan • Organize • Direct • Coordinate • Control	• Plan • Organize • Direct • Coordinate • Control
TIME FRAMES	• Continuous operation with no time limits	• Continuous change functions ... with periodic new vision development and implementation
ORGANIZATION TYPE	• Mechanistic form of traditional hierarchy	• Organic form of traditional hierarchy
SYSTEM LEADERSHIP	• CEO and COO	• CEO, Executive Team and Program Management
SYSTEM INTEGRATION	• Same Top Management Leadership team for both Management Systems	• Same Top Management Leadership team for both Management Systems
SYSTEM PARTICIPANTS	• All employees of company	• Selected employees; subject-matter-experts (SME); then all employees of the company
PARTICIPANT COMPETENCES	• Dependable role performance	• Spontaneous innovative performance[15]

Figure 1.12: Two Management Systems with Different Attributes

---

[15] Katz and Kahn, The Social Psychology of Organizations, 1978

In our writing so far, we have attempted to describe the New Paradigm of two Management Systems operating side-by-side in a business. We have also spelled out the functions and disciples that are the engine of the Change-the-Business Management System. Now that we know what is needed in an organizational change, all we have to do is implement, so that the New Paradigm will become the way a company operates on a day-to-day basis.

Part Two:
Implementing
the New Paradigm

Chapter Two

Implementing OPM in the Modern Enterprise: A General Model

Is this a typical Implementation?

What follows in this short first section is largely "tongue in cheek," but we probably have all seen something that looks familiar when the "change of the month" flag goes up outside the executive suite!

Early Phase: Intrigue with OPM

1. Intrigue with the subject of "OPM"
2. Immersion in the details of OPM
3. Attack of the IT and non-IT Vendors who say "they have all the OPM answers!"
4. Loss of vision of the purpose of OPM during the head-long chase into the details and complexity of the OPM project
5. Development of an urgent need to "do OPM to something" . . . anything!

Middle Phase: Infatuation with OPM

1. Broad-side approach to OPM with the latest project management technology
2. "Since we are implementing the tools, we're going to tackle all processes right now!"
3. Taking OPM Management for a spin . . .

4. OPM overload . . . followed by saturation
5. "Whoa!" . . . The beginning of organizational pushback . . .

Last Phase: Implementation . . . followed by Implosion!

1. Many OPM "projects" started all at once . . . "If it moves, OPM it!"
2. OPM IT systems that are now implemented . . . but not used
3. Confusion: "Just what were we trying to do anyway?"
4. Search, pursuit and capture of the instigator of all this effort!
5. Whose idea was this anyway?

The Needed Perspective for Implementing any Change Including OPM

A common and sometimes useful way of thinking about introducing a new way of thinking and acting in an organization is shown in Figure 2.1. While the figure clearly communicates that implementing the OPM is the goal, the diagram itself tends to focus attention on the definition and explanation of OPM as a means of improving change performance. Implementers who have the view below tend to construct their implementation road maps almost exclusively of communication and intensive training on OPM concepts and techniques . . . which turn out to be necessary but inadequate steps for an effective implementation.

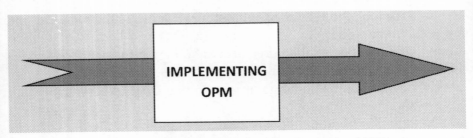

Figure 2.1: Focusing Attention on the Contents of OPM

The implementation process can be better seen and understood by using Figure 2.2 to visualize the change. The central idea in organizational change is to take an organization that is operating in one way (without OPM) and to transition that organization to a new way of operating (with OPM). Such a transition would clearly require more than training and communication . . . more moving parts would be involved such as work processes, technology, job descriptions, etc. It really is as simple as that . . . and as complex too, because organizations have many "moving parts" that will be involved in a transition to a new way of doing business.

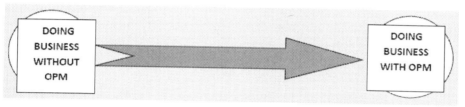

Figure 2.2: Focusing Attention on the Needed Organizational Change

Overview of the Three Phases of Implementation of Organizational Project Management

Unfortunately, one does not wake up one morning to find that OPM is in place and fully operational. If that were only the case, life would be much easier. Instead what advocates of OPM find is that they have a long journey to make OPM a part of everyday business in their company. Moving from doing business without use of OPM to operating daily taking advantage of OPM is a real trip. Fortunately there is at least a high level, three-phase Roadmap (Figures 2.3 and 2.4).

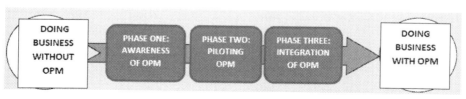

Figure 2.3: The Three Phases of Implementation of OPM

• Phase One: Awareness of OPM and Education about an Intended Change

This phase is simple enough. Many folks in a company may never have heard of Organizational Project Management. Phase one takes on the task of communication and public relations, as well as some training to make sure over time that organization member have a basic understanding of what OPM is, how it can be used, how it can be implemented and last but not least, how operating the company with the benefits of OPM can make things better not only for the company but for the work force as well.

We will go into more detail about this phase later in this chapter but for now, two important ideas stand out. First, who first becomes aware of the nature and benefits of OPM matters a lot, as you can imagine. So while awareness and education is an organization-wide effort, the organization's OPM advocates must pay special attention to the executive team, those folks who may be most difficult to reach and, frequently, who are the most "hard of learning."

The last step in Phase one is critical. In that last step decision makers make an assessment of OPM's value to the company and, if seen as potentially valuable, complete what amounts to a business plan for Phase Two: OPM Trial and Pilot Projects, complete with projections of the economics of running, say, a half-dozen pilot projects, each focused on using OPM in a change initiative. Why not just start a few pilots, you say? Well, you could, but the idea is to make the transition from Phase One to Phase Two a formal business action with top management being there to "cut the ribbon" and to wish the organization well in Phase Two.

• Phase Two: Trial and the Conducting of Pilot Change Projects.

The trial phase has two main objectives: first is to "do and learn" from each pilot project completed and to gain business value from each completed pilot. This phase sounds easy enough until OPM advocates, or appointed change leaders, begin to target specific work processes for improvement using aspects of OPM. The obstacle that is usually the toughest is to convince managers to take time away from an already busy business life and to participate in a pilot project while they continue doing their day jobs of running their business.

Completing a pilot project (that may take several months and cost in the millions nowadays) is tough enough but usually manageable. The tough part, the part most difficult to get pilot team members involved in is the "learning" that is supposed to be a prime reason for doing the pilot. Without clear learning objectives set at the beginning of the pilot, without having learning tasks built into the project plan, and without disciplined supervision of the project managers, the learning part of the pilots will take a very-back seat to completing the technical and work process parts of the pilots. What are the pilot teams supposed to learn during the pilot? The teams are supposed to be learning just about everything . . . with special attention to the following:

- How to do the planning for a pilot to ensure that the pilot project finishes with OPM ready to be used in an improved work process . . .
- How long it takes to get OPM applied to a pilot project, what project steps take the most time, where in the project are the delays and the surprises?
- How is it to manage a project team whose members still have a day job (if they are part-time team members) or hopefully have a day job waiting for them (if they are full-time team members)?

Again, a critical last step in Phase Two is to prepare a business plan for Phase Three of the OPM implementation. At least OPM advocates will know more than they did when they completed the last business plan . . . and their economic projections should be sharper. This business plan, done at the end of Phase Two, is really the business plan for the enterprise initiative aimed at gaining wide-spread use and value from OPM.

Top management must be integral to completing and buying off on the plan . . . or it is probably best to continue gaining some business value from pilot projects rather than to start the intense effort of Phase Three that will last more than a year and impact just about every employee (and customer).

• Phase Three: Integration of a Change into the organization

Implementing all the parts of OPM is both a time-consuming and challenging endeavor. A valid formula or framework will need to be used to identify all the moving parts that need to change and then to change them in an organized and disciplined way. The good news is that many of the moving parts can be altered in parallel and with the right level of leadership, resources, and discipline.

Despite some gains in business value from the pilot projects of Phase Two, the real pay-off comes when OPM is operational . . . and kept in place by committed leadership and an effective PMO.

Difficulty of the three Phases—from "Difficult" to "Much More Difficult"

Phases One and Two are busy and work-intensive, but compared to Phase Three, they are a cake walk. The degree of difficulty for Phase Three jumps at least ten-fold . . . the mechanisms or road maps to complete Phase Three are few and far between. Fortunately, we have outlined a general roadmap in this book.

Despite the best of intentions, some companies that embark on an OPM journey wind up "stuck in Phase Two." Being stuck there is not the result organizations want, but Phase Two, especially a continuing Phase Two, can have real value for the organization as more and more pilot projects are completed in different part of the organization. Each pilot, if successfully completed, could make some things better, and a series of pilots can cover a lot of ground. However, covering a lot of ground is a far cry from moving through Phase Two to a true OPM-based enterprise.

PHASE ONE: AWARENESS & EDUCATION

- Understand the OPM movement
- Develop rationale /case for change to OPM
- Select framework for Transitioning to OPM
- Develop OPM champions
- Conduct informal OPM assessment
- Conduct OPM awareness / education
- **Develop business case for Phase II: OPM Trial / Pilot Projects**
- **Gate: Business Case Accepted?**

PHASE TWO: PILOT PROJECTS

- Formally assess OPM needs
- Pinpoint strategic OPM targets
- Develop pilot projects to "learn and do"
- Conduct just-in-time OPM training of pilot teams
- Make sure pilot results are put into action
- Launch other OPM projects ... based on need and visibility
- **Developed business case for Phase III: Organization wide OPM**
- **Gate: Business Case accepted?**

PHASE THREE: WIDE-SPREAD INTEGRATION

- Develop / communicate a detailed OPM vision
- Develop implementation plans / timeline /measures / goals....
- Incorporate OPM measures/objectives into goals and rewards
- Modify work processes for OPM effectiveness
- Acquire, formalize, integrate OPM tools
- Measure OPM results
- **Identify and maintain a supportive environment for OPM**

Figure 2.4: The Three Phases of Implementation of OPM in More Detail

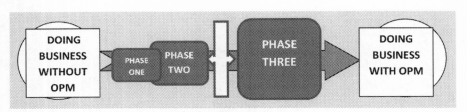

Figure 2.5: Phase Three Requires Much More Effort

Remember the Context

In case we have not painted a picture of the difficulty of Phase Three in realistic enough terms, we might remind ourselves of the context of OPM implementation. As shown in Figure 2.6 below, Phase Three is the final act of implementing the second management system in the organization. Speaking of difficulty, the final implementation of an organizational change like the one required for OPM has been described as like changing an engine on a Boeing 747 while midway between Los Angeles and New York!

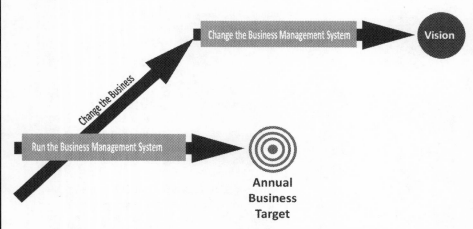

Figure 2.6: The Context for Phase Three of Implementation

Completing Phase Three requires a definite shift in thinking and the use of implementation principles that are valid (i.e., that will produce desired results). Therefore, before launching this book's deep dive into Phase Three, time should be spent to prepare for that Phase. The next two Chapters will explain the shift by covering "organizational change mechanics" and a metaphor that will make the implementation of OPM more understandable and far easier to complete.

Chapter Three

Implementing an Organizational Change

Today's leaders must be able to
- Run the business well . . . all the time and
- Change the business well . . . every time.

The Management Imperative to Lead Change . . . and Change Projects

Organizational change is happening in almost every business organization, but success has been elusive. Senior leaders in business know that changes are needed not only system-wide but in their own organizations. They know the kinds of changes their organizations need and when they are needed. And certainly they know that the responsibility for change rests squarely on their shoulders. Take, for example, the kinds of changes that managers in a recent survey said they would need to make to continue the success of their companies.

- New strategic alliance or joint venture
- Cross border acquisition or merger
- Shifting sourcing (labor to China, innovation to Germany or US)
- China as a part of Growth Strategy
- Growing customer base and accessing local talent
- Being more responsive to customer demands and competitor threat
- Uncertainty about economic growth
- Investing to ensure a supply of future talent
- Shared investment with government to create and foster a skilled work force

- Ensuring financial security of the firm

Source: PwC 15th Annual Global CEO Survey

To this we must add the unending and unflattering statistics of project management success. Many projects continue to fail or to be significantly challenged when it comes to cost and schedule. The numbers refuse to improve significantly, even with thousands and thousands of additional certified project managers (PMPs), better methodologies, techniques, and tools. The reason is simple. Projects continue to grow in size and complexity, defying the efforts of even the best project management professionals working in the absence of an effective OPM environment.

Business executives know that their boards of directors expect more than day-to-day performance; those board members expect the executives they support to make the changes needed to ensure a profitable, long-term, future for the organization in which the owners have invested. In short, today's business leaders must both run the business well all the time and change the business well every time. And that is where Organizational Project Management comes in!

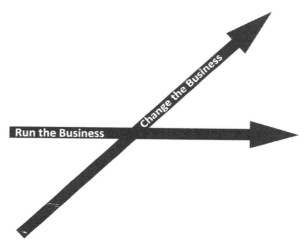

Figure 3.1: Run the Business, Change the Business

Changing the way an organization works is no longer an occasional exercise; change is no longer the exception . . . it is now the rule. Changing the way an organization operates is central to organizational improvement and to the enhancement of business or organizational results. In today's world, change management is the most important role of organizational leadership. Change, in fact, can be looked at as "the natural order of things" for a business enterprise.

The paramount problem with organizational change today is that change initiatives are rarely successful. The often-quoted statistic is that only 30% of organizational change attempts meet management expectations of transitioning the organization from one way of doing business to another. Three reasons for poor change performance are apparent. Today's business leaders lack:

1. **A Change-the-business mind set**. A key reason that change projects fail is because the managers who lead them lack both a change-the-business mindset and a change-the-business skill set. Most managers have spent the majority of careers in running a business, not changing one, and consequently they lack the knowledge and the experience needed to lead organizational change successfully. In many cases, managers do not consider the implementation of Organizational Project Management as a major business change, which could not be further from the truth!

2. **An understanding of the formula for organizational change:** The management community as a whole lacks an understanding of the moving parts that make up an organization; moving parts that must be managed in order for successful change to happen. Change projects are not easy to understand or manage . . . what is needed is a universal understanding of ways to successfully complete change projects. In short most managers lack an understanding of the formula for organizational change. And, when it comes to Organizational Project Management, virtually all moving parts of the organization will be eventually impacted by its implementation.

3. **Appreciation for and competence in Project management:** Managers who spend their careers running a business do not necessarily develop skill or experience in project management thinking or use. Consequently many organizational changes are not treated like a project with a fixed beginning and end, or, at the other extreme, change initiatives are treated as projects, but chartered with unmanageable scope or complexity. Finally, if today's managers lack appreciation for and competence in Project Management, just imagine how far behind they are in appreciating OPM!

These three issues must be addressed in change management literature as well as in the minds of today's business leaders, or organizations will flounder under the waves of change confronting them. A goal of this book is to resolve all three issues.

The Needed Perspective for Implementing OPM

The starting place for successful organizational change is with the understanding of what an organization is and what organizational change means. We are not implying that people who work in today's business organizations don't understand them . . . of course they do . . . to the level needed to do a good job of running the day-to-day business.

But we have found that most managers and employees do not understand organizations at the level needed to lead effective organizational change. For example, it would be hard to say that I don't understand my car. Of course I understand my car! I drive it to work every day, I ensure that it's taken care of; I even play with it occasionally on a deserted, winding road. I understand it—as a transportation system or a toy. But the truth is that I don't understand very much about my car as a system of moving parts. When I open the hood of my car to peer inside, I quickly realize that I am ignorant of my car at "open hood" level. I've always counted on somebody else to take care of the stuff under the hood to keep my car running.

Successful organizational change requires us to know something about what an organization has "under the hood." It is critical that we understand the organization from a structural or systems point of view. We need to learn something about the many moving parts of organizations—like a driver would have to learn some mechanics if he had to take over responsibility for maintaining his car. In today's world of work, business managers must be able to both run the organization to get today's business done and to get under the hood to change the organization so that it will be ready to do tomorrow's business as well.

The way any organization (or a car) works at a given point in time is the direct and inescapable result of the configuration of its moving parts. An organization has four main components or categories of moving parts that are vitally involved in every change.

1. **Vision** . . . the organization's sense of what it is and where it is trying to go, as in its business model . . . the unifying idea and spirit that makes up the organization's identity.

2. **Work processes** . . . the many steps that organization members (and machines) must take on a daily basis to satisfactorily produce the organization's products and services.

3. **Facilities, equipment and technology (FET)** . . . the organization's plant and facilities along with its tools, equipment, software, that organization members use in the organization's work processes

4. **Performance management system** . . . the organization's mechanisms for engaging workers to follow work processes, use the provided tools to enact the sense of direction or business model (e.g., job descriptions, training, performance appraisal and compensation systems, etc.)[16]

---

[16] The moving parts of an organization have been identified by no less than a veritable "who's who of OD" serving as the Board of Editors of the widely-accepted Jossey-Bass/Pfeiffer series of books on Organization Development: David Bradford is senior lecturer in Organizational Behavior, Graduate School of Business, Stanford University; W. Warner Burke is Professor of Psychology, Columbia University; Edith Whitfield Seashore is organizational consultant and co-founder of AUNTL Master's

An organization cannot change from one way of doing business to another without changes in its moving parts. Organizational change requires physical alteration of these four categories of components or there will be no change at all. Calling these needed alterations "requirements" may help managers see that the needed alterations of an organization's moving parts are not optional; they are a necessity! (See Figure 3.2)

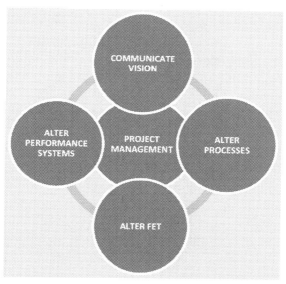

Figure 3.2: The major categories of an organization's moving parts

Requirements for Successful organizational change

Successful organizational change depends on the use of the change formula made up of the following "moving parts" . . . or requirements:

Program in Organization Development; Robert Tannenbaum is emeritus Professor of Development of Human Systems, University of California, Los Angeles; Christopher G. Worley, Director of the MSOD Program at Pepperdine University; and Shaolin Zhang is senior member of Organization Development for Motorola (China) Electronics Ltd.

---

1. *Communicating a new and exciting vision,*
2. *Creatively altering work processes,*
3. *Incorporating robust and powerful FET, and*
4. *Restructuring challenging roles for employees and preparing them to take those roles.*

Successful change also depends on the use of disciplined project management that ensures that all the organization's moving parts are prepared and positioned properly for a new and better way of doing business.

These four alterations make up what we call the requirements for a successful transition from one way of operating or doing business to another. We also see the list of moving parts as a sort of "formula for organizational change." Attempting organizational change without a new vision or without altering any of the other three moving parts will result in a contribution to the "70%" statistic of change attempts that do not meet management expectations!

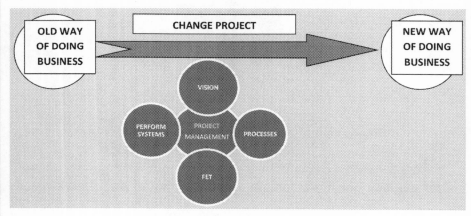

Figure 3.3: Organizational change as a project

Understanding organizational change as a series of change projects

The old question asks, "How do you eat an elephant?" And the answer follows, "One bite at a time!" And how do you change an organization? The answer is "one successful project at a time." Changing an organization is a big job, and trying to make the change as one single project is just too broad to be manageable. Successful organizational change depends on the completion of several well-thought-out change projects that, when completed, have produced the new way of doing business.

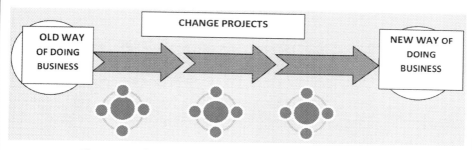

Figure 3.4: Organizational change as a series of projects

The formula for each of the change projects is a fractal[17] of the formula for changing the entire organization. That is, each change project requires the use of the same actions used in the general formula (as shown in the Figure 3.4). The scope of these "smaller change projects" will be driven by the same change formula even though they will not cover as much ground as an entire organizational change. The smaller scope of these projects, therefore, can be easier to manage and complete successfully.

---

[17] A fractal has the feature of "self-similarity." For instance, it is easily understood by the analogy of zooming in with a lens on the digital image of cell to uncover finer, previously invisible, new structure. If this is done on fractals, however, no new detail appears; nothing changes and the same pattern repeats over and over, or for some fractals, nearly the same pattern reappears over and over.

Identifying the change projects that will drive the organizational change

Imagine a regional hospital that decides to shift their focus to seniors and to cancer patients. The shift was decided after careful analysis of the latest regional census. Making this change would clearly give the hospital a new identity and image in the healthcare marketplace . . . and require many dollars and resources. Imagine that a savvy executive team decides to manage the implementation of the new strategy with a set of change projects rather than as one massive initiative (Figure 3.5).

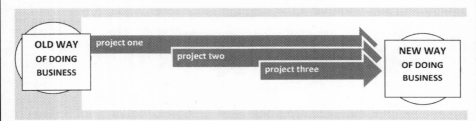

Figure 3.5: Organizational change as a series of parallel projects

This example is so simple that the potential change projects are practically obvious. But for the sake of the example, imagine the executives using the organizational change formula as a guide to developing the first set of change projects.

Formula Elements/Requirements	Change Projects
• Communicate the vision	• **Identity Project:** Marketing, Public Relations, and internal communication

• Alter work processes	• **Scheduling Project:** Altering the automated scheduling system to accommodate chemo and radiation treatments
• Alter FET (facilities, tools, etc.)	• **Radiology Project:** Addition of radiology facility and equipment
• Alter performance management	• **Geriatric Project:** Attract and integrate physicians into a geriatrics treatment practice • **Cancer Project:** Attract and integrate physicians into a cancer treatment practice

This example shows quite a few change projects that could be generated after some careful thought. This list of five projects will not be enough to complete the desired organizational change, but it might be more than an organization can successfully complete in a year's time, and it will be up to the executive team to select what they believe will be a full slate of projects for an upcoming year. We urge change leaders to include only a few projects that can be done well rather than many projects that can drag on or be marginally successful.

Identifying the change projects within the change projects

So now that we have identified the slate of change projects for the upcoming year, what do we do next? Once again the same organizational change formula must be used, but this time the formula must be applied to each and every project. That's right, the same formula works at the project level as well as the organizational level.

The figure below shows the formula again in use for two of the five example change projects the regional hospital has elected to pursue for the upcoming year. Taking the radiology example, two visions would be communicated to the radiology staff: the overall hospital vision of becoming a regional cancer center and the vision of how the radiology practice will be operating at the future target date. Work processes would also need to be considered at two levels: at the hospital level where we understand radiology to logically fit in a cancer center, and at the department level where we consider the needed work processes inside a radiology department. The same flow would apply to the second example: the Chemo Training program.

Change Project	Formula Elements	Radiology Change Projects
Radiology Project	Communicate the vision	Communicate the radiology vision to department members
	Alter work processes	Adopt radiology clinical pathways (i.e., clinical work processes)
	Alter FET (facilities, tools)	Purchase and install radiology assets
	Alter performance management	Identify radiology staff needs and hire needed physicians/technicians

Change Project	Formula Elements	Chemo Training Change Projects
Chemo Training Project	Communicate the vision	Communicate the chemo nursing vision
	Alter work processes	Amend nursing procedure manual for chemo

	Alter FET (facilities, tools)	Install sterilization facility
	Alter performance management	Purchase vendor training for nursing and alter nurse job descriptions

Notice how "projects generate projects" as action plans are developed for a desired change at both the organization and department levels. At this point, the magnitude of moving parts in an organizational change can be seen more clearly . . . along with some of the reasons why 70% of change projects come up short. The need for some mechanism for keeping track of all the moving parts is obvious. The need for formal project management of the moving parts is now apparent. The use of strong project management has saved many organizational change initiatives. Project management based on generally-accepted principles will be invaluable in an organizational change like the one in our example. Once OPM is in place, the PMO will provide the necessary leadership to increase the chances that these change projects are successful.

Organizational change can be overwhelming in both complexity and scope. By focusing on completing four or five concrete change projects in a year's time, busy executives will know they are making progress toward the organization's vision for the future. With OPM in place, success will become even more probable and not just possible. Meet each of the requirements (i.e., make each project a success) and you have a successful change.

> *Now what is the point again?*
> *Nail each project (i.e., make each project a success), and you will have successful organizational change. Fail to nail each project . . . and success goes out the window!*

A universal metaphor for understanding organizational change[18]

We have had very good luck in using metaphors and analogies to communicate about change with managers and students as well. We searched for years to find a simple metaphor for organizational change, and we finally found one . . . one that was right under our noses all the time. The idea that an organization can be thought of as a "continuous one-act play performed by a theatre company" works well as a change metaphor and will be used throughout the book.

A change vision, for example, can be characterized as a "script for a play." And the idea of organizational change can be likened to a theatre company transitioning to a new play. Vision—script, get it? Well, of course, everybody gets it . . . and more. We all know that a play has a script (vision), roles (work processes), costumes/settings (tools), and actor contracts (performance agreements), rehearsals (training) and so on. The beauty of this theater metaphor is that almost everybody is familiar with the workings of a play. They already know that a script is needed (a mechanical), roles must be assigned, costumes must be fitted, contracts re-written and signed, etc.

Once the ideas of changing the play and changing an organization are "connected" in the minds of managers, the needed steps for organizational change are very easy to explain and, therefore, to plan and execute. Since all world cultures have the concept of theatre in them, we have been able to work with the metaphor world-wide.

> *The guiding metaphor*
> *An organization can be thought of as a theater company that*
> *gives a satisfying performance to an audience of customers.*

Before discounting this metaphor as childish, consider that most of us get up each morning, put on our work clothes (costumes), travel to our

---

[18] From the book **Change is the Rule . . .** by Winford E Dutch Holland, Dearborn Press, Chicago, 2000

company (the theater), walk into our office (the set) and execute our jobs (roles) according to the organizations' goals and objectives (the script) to deliver products and/or services to customers (the audience)—until it's time to go home to start all over again the next day.

Once the theater metaphor is mastered, it becomes easy to understand a critically important concept in organizational change—that organizations can be seen as structured, systems with concrete components or moving parts that must work and change together.

Using the theater metaphor, we can more clearly see and understand an organization's four primary structural components:

- **Vision . . . like the storyline and script of a play.** The vision is the organization's sense of what it is and where it is trying to go, as in its business model

- **Work processes . . . like the roles in the play.** Work processes are the steps that organization members must take on a daily basis to produce the organization's products and services

- **FET . . . like the costumes and sets.** FET includes the organization's facilities along with tools, equipment, and software. Workers use the organization's FET to enable work processes

- **Performance management system . . . like the actors' contracts and rehearsals.** The performance management system is the organization's mechanism for engaging workers to follow work processes, using the provided FET to bring the organization's vision to life.

In our experience, the most difficult part of organizational change for many companies is seeing that change is designed to alter the roles that people play in the organization, not to attempt to "alter people" themselves. In our experience, failure to grasp the idea that change hinges on altering roles and subsequent performance agreements that we make with employees, is a major cause of unsuccessful organizational change. With OPM successfully in place, this situation can change fairly dramatically, as the Enterprise PMO will routinely help the organization with its primary structural components. But in the meantime, we need to make sure that OPM itself is implemented first!

Understanding organizational change as "changing the play"

In the theater metaphor, organizational change would be the equivalent of a theater company transitioning from the daily performance of an existing play to the daily performance of a new play that starts next week or next month, requiring the physical transition of actor roles and contracts, costumes, sets, etc.

Imagine a theater company that has been performing nightly Shakespeare's Romeo and Juliet transitioning to "Cats." The transition to the new play would require many concrete steps to physically distribute the script, alter roles, costumes and set as well as to prepare the specific contracts of the actors . . . and that's all there is to it . . . except for the million other details needed to shut down an award-winning play and replace it with another award-winner.

In the theater, change mastery is critical because no play lasts forever, and the success of the theater company will be determined by its ability to transition from one successful play to another. The same is true in business where no way of operating will last forever, and the long-term survival of the organization will be dependent on making effective transitions from one way of doing business to another.

Many years of experience has confirmed for us that both managers and employees easily grasp the changes needed to transition a theater company from one performance to another—from learning new scripts and parts to changing costumes and sets, all the way to the full dress rehearsals before opening night. Once this theater metaphor is learned, managers and employees alike can easily use it to understand why many changes they have seen went awry!

Using the theatre metaphor to understand the formula for change

Let's use the idea of "theater" to guide our understanding of an organizational change and to preview the five requirements to be covered in detail in the rest of the book. The five requirements below comprise what we think of as the "formula" for organizational change—the steps that must be followed to either "change from one play to another" or "change an organization from one way of doing business to another."

Requirement One: Communicate a vision for the organization

- *If you want to change the play, you must start by selecting and communicating a new script.*

- *If you want to change the way an organization does business, you must start by communicating a new vision of how the organization will need to operate at a selected future time.*

- *If you want to implement OPM, you must start by communicating a vision of how the organization will manage Change-the-Business (CTB/OPM) at a selected future time.*

We have probably all been to a movie or theater production and come out with the evaluation that "the plot was weak" or even "there was no plot!" What we usually mean by that evaluation is that for us the production did not make sense and there was limited attractiveness, fun, or satisfaction. The production just didn't work for us.

A company should also have a "story line or plot" that gets executed by the people in the organization. Sometimes it is a good story line (Windows software or Apple's iPAD) and sometimes it is not (the New Coke). Organizations use different words or terms to describe their story lines or plots. Story lines are called many things: vision, mission, purpose, strategy, game plan, direction . . . or any one of a dozen other terms. The hottest new title for an organization's story line is the mind twister . . . "Value Proposition!"

Our position is simple, we don't care what an organization calls its story line . . . it is just critical that the organization have a winning one . . . and that everyone knows what it is! Our interest and idea is again simple; when an organization wants to change, one of the four things it will need to modify or alter is its story line, or its vision.

In a theater production, detailed written scripts are used . . . from which actors can read or conclude the story line. In organizations, much of the story line is not written down for everybody to read. Even in those cases where the organization has a written and posted Mission, Vision, and/or Strategy, much of the story line is implicit . . . understood by many but not written down. In later sections of this book, we will have recommendations about making more of the organization's story line explicit to support organizational transitions. The bottom line is this; if we want the world to see a different story line from our organization, we will need to develop and detail that new story line . . . or we will have nothing to use as a guide for an organizational change.

Requirement Two: Alter work processes

- *If you want to transition to a new play, you must select the roles for the new play.*

- *If you want to transition a business organization, old work processes (e.g., the way customer complaints are handled, shipping instructions, etc.) must be altered . . . or new processes must be created that will enable the new way of doing business to be achieved.*

- *If you want to transition the organization to the use of OPM, old work processes (formal or informal) used to "manage organizational change" (e.g., the way change task forces are assigned and directed, the way portfolios of project are managed, etc.) musts be altered . . . or new processes must be added*

Theatergoers can easily identify parts or roles in a play as different actors behave differently on stage. That is, each actor is seen taking specific steps, saying certain lines, hiding his derringer up his shirt sleeve, and interacting with other actors in certain scenes. If the theatergoer were to return to the theater to see the same play some months later, she would likely see actors performing those same roles all over again (the actors might have been replaced but the roles would not). In organizational terms, the parts that employees play are the daily work processes that produce the organization's goods and services.

An observer could follow different workers in an organization to see or even document the steps taken by that worker over the course of a time cycle (a work-day, week, or month). Following all the workers in an organization could theoretically allow the observer to see all of the organization's work processes. An observer who sees all of an organization's work processes is likely to conclude, in a well-managed organization, at least, that all the processes seem to be focused on bringing about the purpose of the organization.

In fact, the results that are produced by any organization at a given point in time are directly related to both the kind and performance level of all of the organization's work processes. So, from an organizational change perspective, if we want customers to experience a different story line from our organization, we will need to modify or alter our organization's work processes . . . or the customers will see nothing different at!!

Requirement Three: Alter facilities, equipment, and Tools (FET)

- *If you want to transition to a new play, you must select the theater, build the props, and fit costumes for the actors.*

- *If you want to transition a business organization, old equipment must be altered and/or new equipment must be bought to support the organization's new work processes.*

- *If you want to transition your organization to the use of OPM, equipment/software must be altered or purchased to support the work processes of CTB/OMP (Visioning, Portfolio, Program, Project Management, Change Engineering).*

Theatergoers see props and costumes when they go to a performance. They don't see all of the theater or the "behind-the-scenes equipment," but they know they are there based on what happens on the stage . . . scenes change, actors dangle, or dance into and out of rooms that were not on stage in the last scene. For many plays to make sense to the audience, certain props or costumes are needed. While props and costumes don't "make the play," they clearly are indispensable parts of the whole . . . and the clarity of the story line would suffer without them. Imagine for a moment that a "fresh behind the ears" director decides to perform "Cats" with both male and female actors dressed in business suits (or scuba gear)!

Just as in the theater, organizations require the use of FET to execute the work processes needed to produce the products and services that fulfill the organization's purpose or direction. For the sake of brevity we will use the word "FET" to represent the facilities, plants, equipment, tools, computer systems, the organization uses to do its day-to-day work. As an example, a local orthopedic radiology shop uses an office building, furnishings, x-ray equipment, stands for patients to stand on or beds for them to lie on, and computer hardware and software to bring to life its work processes and to make possible the development and testing of its primary product . . . visible images for physicians to read.

And just as in the theater, some of an organization's FET is visible . . . and some is, for all intents and purposes, invisible. Invisible tools include "what's behind the walls, under the floor, and in the ceiling" as well as what's inside the computer. Software turns out to be an indispensable tool in today's business organizations, and software is, to a large degree, invisible to workers except for what they see on their computer screens. Months of alterations of an inventory control system can go along un-noticed while major alterations to the positioning of machine tools would be hard to miss. For an organization to change the way it does business through its work processes, the organization's FET must be altered, whether it be visible or invisible.

Requirement Four: Alter performance systems

- *If you want to change the play, you must put actors under contract for specific roles for the new play and rehearse them until they can perform their roles perfectly.*

- *If you want to change an organization, workers must be under new agreements to perform to altered, detailed job descriptions and goals . . . and workers must be trained in the new or altered work processes and accompanying FET.*

- *If you want to implement CTB/OPM in the organization, workers involved with managing change must be under agreement to manage change in the new way; they should have altered, detailed job descriptions and goals that include managing change, training in OPM; and they should be evaluated on how well they manage change, etc.*

We clearly see the actors when we sit in the theater. It is the actors who bring the story line of the play to life. But what we see is the "performance" given by the actors. We know as we sit in the theater that every person we see on stage is a professional actor portraying her role and speaking her lines from the script. We also know that the actor is under contract to do the play (or she would not be there!), and that the performance we are seeing is only possible after the actor accepts, studies and rehearses her part.

We see workers in organizations as actors with assigned parts who are under an agreement to give a performance for their organization. We see the training that the worker has received as akin to the study and rehearsal done by the actor to be able to perform in a play. The workers in our example radiology practice will have been trained and certified in different roles in the organization—like radiologist assistants (RAs), nurse practitioners (NPs), radiology practitioner assistants (RPAs),—using the tools of the practice, to produce images for the physicians who request them.

The concrete, moving parts of the organization that we use in transition projects are worker agreements and training. We call these moving parts the "performance management system" that leaders of an organization use to ensure that workers will be ready, willing, and able to complete all the needed work for organizational success. In the theater, for example, the performance management system would be similar . . . with specific contracts for actors (calling for performance in an assigned role for a certain amount of compensation) and planned rehearsals to ensure that the actors had developed their parts and were able to perform as required with the entire theatre company.

Beyond the worker agreement, the actor receives guidance from the Director on some of the finer points of the performance of the part. The Director has the responsibility to tell the story in the play through the performance of the actors. And the actors have the responsibility to act the part to the best of their ability to ensure a successful performance. In organizations, workers have the responsibility to act out their assigned roles with the assistance of a manager who is responsible for blending a number of roles into the performance needed to meet the organizational goals called for by the new way of doing business.

Requirement Five: Manage the change as a project

- *If you want to transition to a new play, you must manage all the "moving parts" of the transition as a project: closely following a master schedule for handing out the script, for signing actors, for fitting costumes, for conducting rehearsals, and so on.*

- *If you want to transition an organization to a new way of doing business, the alterations of all moving parts should be treated as a project: closely following a schedule for communicating the vision, altering work processes and FET, training workers, and so on.*

- *Now get this, you must use OPM to implement OPM! If you want to transition your organization to the use of OPM, the communication and the alteration of all moving parts should be treated like a project: closely following a schedule for communicating the vision of OPM, altering work processes and FET for managing Change-the-Business, etc.*

Even though actors are clear on the new play they are planning to perform, they need a day-to-day transition plan and schedule to get ready to perform. And even though organizational workers are clear on the vision that is to be implemented, they too need day-by-day or week-by-week action plans to guide them through the many steps of organizational change. Employees need action plans that tell them "what to do on each Monday morning . . ." to go forward with the coordinated implementation of the new way of doing business.

These action plans must be a part of a critical path project management plan and master schedule that lays out all the transition work to be done for the organizational change. Critical to the action planning requirement is the translation of action plans on a weekly or monthly basis for all involved managers and employees so that they are clear on both their roles in transitioning to the new organization as well as playing a new or altered role in that new organization. Failure to keep action plans up to date and communicated would be like the director who does not lay out and communicate detailed plans and schedules for the reading for new roles, signing of contracts, fittings for new costumes, rigging of new props, and dates for rehearsals.

The challenge in this action planning requirement is to ensure that all of the required modifications to vision, work processes, FET and performance agreements have been completed in a thorough and comprehensive manner. While it may be a technical challenge to keep track of all of the needed alterations, particularly if the organization is large, it is technically not difficult to find out exactly where the organization is in organizational change.

You know where you are

Knowing where we are in transitioning a theater company to a new play or transitioning an organization to a new way of doing business is a matter of auditing the status of the change projects that have been established—and dealing with the reality of what we find:

- **Requirement One: Either the vision for the company's new way of doing business has been developed and documented . . . or it has not!** Either managers have had the opportunity to discuss and question the new vision and make it their own . . . or they have not! Each member of the organization has been personally briefed on what will be the new way of working . . . or he/she has not . . . and so on.

- **Requirement Two: Either work processes have been altered . . . or they have not!** New procedures to allow people to follow those altered processes have been written and distributed . . . or they have not! The old processes and their supporting procedures have been dismantled and destroyed . . . or they have not!

- **Requirement Three: Either the new FET is on board and working . . . or it is not!** Either the guidelines for operating the new FET have been written and distributed . . . or they have not. Either the old FET and its operating instructions have been removed and/or disabled . . . or they have not!

- **Requirement Four: Either the performance agreement for each and every manager and employee impacted by the change has been altered and negotiated with him/her . . . or it has not!** Either each and every manager and employee has been trained on the new processes and new FET . . . or they have not! And so on!!

- **Requirement Five: Either there is a master schedule of actions that need to be taken to meet the other four requirements . . . or there is not.** Each and every member of the workforce knows what change actions to take this week . . . or they do not!

Be ready for mind-clearing examples to introduce each chapter

In the chapters that follow, be on the look-out for "Mind-Clearing Examples." Such examples will be of a real-world situation that would be "absurd" to find in a theater company . . . but that might be "common place" to find in the real world of business.

> **Mind-Clearing Example—Imagine a Director who is communicating the new play to the theater company. He says, "Rather than give each of you that inch-thick script for the new play, look at this. I have prepared a couple of succinct PowerPoint slides that will explain the entire play in two minute flat!"**

The two-slide slide show would be an absurd idea in the theater . . . and yet somehow it feels familiar in business as top management hands out the "seven key one-liners that describe their vision for the future." Such Mind-Clearing Examples will set the stage for the material to be covered in each of the chapters about successfully transitioning an organization to a new way of doing business.

This book and how it might be used

This book on changing or transitioning organizations to a new way of operating is all about doing organizational change successfully. This book is not about the psychological concepts and theories that underlie organizational change;[19] it's about the real-world practical actions that must be taken to make each organizational change successful.

Where do these practical actions come from? They come from the many things learned over time about leading an organizational change; from the literature of management, change, and the behavioral sciences; from the principles of project management, from the lessons learned in

---

[19] While psychological concepts and theories that underlie organizational change will not be discussed explicitly in this book's content, you can know that such concepts have been "baked into" the actions recommended in the book.

the real world of organizational change. These practical actions come from those organizations that have mastered change and that have demonstrated time and again that they can successfully transition their organizations to new ways of working—on target, on time, and on budget!

First, the action steps in each upcoming chapter are designed to impact the moving parts of an organization and can be used as tasks in a change project's task list and master schedule.[20] Second, a change professional might use this book for its "management and business language" that bridges today's world of business and many behavioral and change concepts. Third, the book might be used to give to managers as a part of a change professional's explanation of how a change project might need to work. And last but not least, the information contained in this book about team composition, meeting agendas, and management scripts might assist a manager or a change professional in planning his/her change work.

As a reader of this book you will learn to guide change—a subject that has not likely been a part of your business education. You will no longer feel lost during organizational change—you will have a road map for change that you can confidently follow. You will know what concrete actions to take and when to take them. You will know what to expect of employees and how to work with them during the change process. You will be able to manage and communicate organizational change in a way that does not seem life- or ego-threatening to organization members.

Best of all, as a reader of this book, you will never again look at organizational change as a mysterious experience to be feared and fought. You will see organizational change as a set of concrete projects, creative acts of leadership than can be completed—on target, on time, and on budget!

20

Summary

In this day and time business organizations are being forced to effectively change faster than they ever have before. In the past most businesses could gradually adapt to external forces that affected their bottom lines. They could simply squeeze out waste, reduce unprofitable services and get by. But in today's world, the magnitude and speed of changing rules won't allow traditional gradual change techniques to be effective. Today's leaders must be able to run the business well all the time and change the business well every time. And, with OPM in place, these leaders will have a much better chance to be successful, as each planned change effort will be part of the OPM activities managed by the Enterprise PMO.

So the two-paragraph summary of this book might be as follows:

This is a book about making organizational change happen successfully by altering an organization's moving parts that affect organizational effectiveness. Disciplined project management along with use of the change formula for altering the moving parts can lead to successful organizational change, while ignoring any part of the formula puts an organizational change at risk.

This book is also about implementing a Change-the-Business Management System, a new way of making and managing changes in an organization by using the discipline of Organizational Project Management (OPM). Disciplined project management along with use of the change formula for altering the moving parts that are associated with Change-the-Business can lead to successful organizational change to OPM, while ignoring any part of the formula puts an organization's way of handling change at risk.

Part Three: Action Steps for Implementing Change and OPM

Introduction

To Chapters Four through Eight

The Recipe Format

Have you ever noticed the format used for food recipes? First you see a list of ingredients. After that, you see the instructions for turning the separate ingredients into the dish. The idea is to explain the bits and pieces (the ingredients) first before any attempt to explain how the bits and pieces will be combined.

We will follow a similar sequence in this book . . . explaining the four major requirements in some detail (communicating the vision of OPM, altering processes for OPM, altering tools and technology, and altering the performance management system that will steer employees toward OPM). After digesting those key chapters (Four through Seven), you will read about the fifth Requirement, using Project Management to combine ingredients for the integration of OPM into an organization (Chapter Eight).

Got it? Requirements (ingredients) first; then instructions on how to project manage the ingredients for an organizational change. That sequence makes sense to us (and to chefs), but perhaps it might be more comfortable for some readers to look at a preview of the Project Management steps.

Preview of Project Management Steps

The general steps to be managed in an organizational change project are as follows:

1. **Chartering the organizational change as a project:** The executive who is commissioning the organizational change should appoint a formal project manager and give him his first assignment of developing the formal charter for the change project. The Project Charter is the executive's and project manager's concise statement of the intent, goals, scope, change budget, limits of and responsibilities for the organizational change.

2. **Development, approval and communication of the master schedule:** The project manager sketches the beginning and desired end points of the organizational change, develops the work breakdown structure and task list, creates the first high-level master schedule, and seeks schedule approval by the executive in charge of the change.

3. **Development of the vision and the case for organizational change:** The change leader launches those activities needed to develop in some detail the vision (i.e., the new way the organization will be doing business in the future) as well as the case for change.

4. **Initial communication of the vision and case for change:** The change leader begins the communication process designed to give the organization a "heads up" to changes that are to be made along with the reasons for those changes.

5. **Identification of change work, that is, the alterations that will need to be made to enable the vision.** The change leader names teams to identify needed alterations in:

    o **Work processes**
    o **FET**
    o **Performance management system** (e.g., worker roles, training, etc.)

6. **Development and communication of a detailed master schedule:** A detailed master schedule is created to show the calendar for completing all needed Change Work.

7. **Alteration of worker roles:** the change leader authorizes bosses to conduct one-on-one contracting with workers for

   o **Starting a new way of working** at the targeted, change-over time
   o **Continuing to perform work** as it is currently done until change-over
   o **Completing the change work** required for change-over (e.g., participating in training, new role development, new equipment break-in, etc.)

8. **Conducting change work:** Many consider this step as the heart of organizational change, where existing work processes are studied, re-designed, and then altered to fit the change vision; where FET is analyzed and actions taken to modify it or to buy and install new FET; and where roles are altered and training delivered, and so on. This step alone can take weeks to months of hard work for some organization members while other members are uninvolved, continuing to conduct today's business as usual . . . until that first training class appears on their schedules.

9. **Verifying all change work:** The change leader ensures all the needed change work has been done, including alteration of work processes, FET, and roles . . . and that tests have been conducted to ensure that all needed alterations have been adequately made.

10. **Changing over to the new way of doing business:** At specific time(s) the various parts of the organization make the switch from doing work the old way to doing work the new way.

11. **Break-in (or learning curve phase) and stabilization:** The change leader aggressively leads during the first few weeks/months of working the new way, during which the organization continues to

learn and make further refinements to work processes, FET, and worker roles to achieve the desired way of doing business.

So much for the preview and now on to the first of the ingredients chapters: Communicating the Vision of a New Way of Doing Business . . . right after we introduce the "case" that will service as our primary example for the book.

Introducing the example case: Killing Two Birds with One Stone

Our example case is of a company that was trying to make two changes at once. First, the company needed to make major changes in the way it worked with its customers. Significant improvement in customer satisfaction was desperately needed if the company was to have a chance to stay competitive.

Second, at the same time, the company was attempting to "improve the way it managed organizational change." The previous two change initiatives the company had initiated had both fizzled before any improvements in business value were realized.

The following case descriptions should be considered "fiction based on truth." The examples do come from a real-world company and are accurate in most ways.

Polymer Plastics Inc. (PPI)

Polymer Plastics Inc. (PPI) was the 5th largest producer of High Density Polyethylene (HDPE) (plastics) and the 9th largest producer of Polypropylene (PP) in the US. Their products went to demanding end users: plastic bottles for Kroger and Wal-Mart; plastic gas tanks for GM, Ford and Chrysler; bottle caps for Coke and Pepsi. Competition was intense from Exxon, Union Carbide, Dow, and Chevron.

After taking over, the new CEO's first realization was that the company was caught between the big guys (big competitors and big customers). The company was not high on their customers' lists of favored vendors because of previous performance. Major changes were needed in the way the business was run, and there was very strong pressure to protect the profits they did have. The CEO had also been briefed by Corporation-level Executives that PPI had a history of failed change attempts.

At that point, the CEO also realized he needed a management method that would (1) allow major changes to be made while (2) he and his senior team gave attention to the existing business.

So the new CEO started with two big problems that would require organizational changes: better customer service and better management of change.

Each of the following chapters will tackle one of the five key components of organizational change, identifying the steps that would be needed to alter that component to allow the organization to transition to a new way of doing business. Examples of each needed step will be given from PPI, the company above.

At the beginning of each example below, you will be able to read about the company's first change initiative: its attempt to improve customer service and satisfaction . . . what and why they did each step and how they did it.

Then you will see the following symbol:

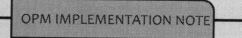

OPM IMPLEMENTATION NOTE

Under that symbol you can read case examples of how PPI was handling its second change initiative: improving their management of change with the implementation of their own version of Organizational Project Management (OPM).

Chapter Four

Communicating a Clear Vision
of a New Way of Doing Business

Mind-Clearing Example—Imagine a Director who says that he and the Producer (the Money Person) have not settled on the script for the next play, but they do know what the performance should look like.

"We see it set in Manhattan with some scenes from upstate New York or South Texas. It should be set in contemporary times with some flashbacks to post World War II or Viet Nam. We think it should be a murder mystery set around a bank heist or a "dangerous love triangle." Some song and dance might go with the bank heist or some outright comedy could be played in the love triangle."

The Director pauses to ask the dazed theater company: "So are you getting a feel for out next play?"

Construct the detailed vision for a new way of doing business

Requirement one, a reasonable place to start, calls for leaders to construct and fully communicate a clear, detailed vision of the organization as they intend for it to be in the future. This vision is the picture of the future that the leader must paint in enough detail for managers and workers alike to understand leadership's intended direction. If the employees of an organization are going to be asked to change, they need to know what that change will look like. And they need as much information about that change as they can get so that they can begin to integrate that picture of the future into their current way of thinking and make suggestions about how to best make the change.

As we described in an earlier chapter, the vision we need to construct can either be for the entire organization undergoing change (e.g., a) or the vision can be for one of the change projects (e.g., implementing a new way of managing change)

Just as a theater company needs a script to understand the new play they are to perform, organization members need a vision to understand the company the leadership wants them to be in the future. And therein lies the rub. Leaders have a tendency to state their vision for the future in terms that are too brief and too sketchy to be fully understood by the workforce. Frequently leaders depend on five or six bullet points on a single page to communicate what they want their organizations to become at some time in the future. The simple truth of the matter is that such a brief and abbreviated vision statement or slogan is totally unsatisfactory as a tool for leading organizational change.

A detailed vision must be constructed so that it captures the real spirit of the desired change and be detailed enough to show the future with

- Organization members (Executives, senior managers, project managers, etc.) . . .
- Performing new work processes (new customer service protocols, new service measurement methods, etc.) . . .
- Using the new facilities, equipment, technology (new shipping software authoring programs) required by those work processes.

Identify and dispel deadly assumptions that will disable communication of the change vision

Before we detail the steps needed to develop and test a vision for the change we want to make, we should examine common assumptions about vision made by many business organizations. Over time, organizations frequently develop assumptions that will, if used, block successful organizational change. These assumptions come into play as soon as managers begin to implement each of the five steps needed to transition an organization to a new way of doing business.

No better example of a change-blocking assumption is the one that disables communication of the vision for the transition to a new way of doing business. The table below shows one of the most deadly assumptions that impacts many if not all organizations attempting change: "people just need to be told about a new direction and they will immediately understand that direction to the level needed to move forward." When we think about that assumption, our experience with life tells us that it is untrue; people have to hear a new message several times before they "get it." Holding such an assumption guarantees that transition will be based on minimal, single-incident under-communication. Such under-communication will likely confuse and bewilder employees and only increase anxiety about an upcoming change.

Step	Deadly Assumptions	Disabling Behavior	Proven Consequences
Requirement One: Communication of the Vision	People just need to be told about a new direction and "they'll get it."	• Minimal, "one-shot" communication • Token communication	• Rumors and miss-information • Anxiety and apprehension about change • Confusion

Change leaders can spot the likely presence of deadly assumptions through conversations heard about what needs to be done to communicate the vision of a new way of doing business. Hearing the suggestion to "stop all this communication planning foolishness and just tell them" calls for the change leader to surface deadly assumptions and to dispel them in any way possible, starting with the proven consequences in the table above.

Take these action steps to complete Requirement One: Communicate the vision

Now we are on to the hard work of communicating the vision that will guide the organization's transition to a new way of doing business. Skip any one of the following five steps and expect expensive delays.

Action steps to communicate the change vision

- 1A: Construct the detailed vision of the new way of doing business
- 1B: Construct the case for change
- 1C: Ensure management understanding and agreement
- 1D: Communicate the vision to the entire organization
- 1E: Ensure employee translation of the vision

Requirement 1A: Construct the detailed vision of the future organization

Mind-Clearing Example—Imagine a Director who introduces his theater company to the next play with the following verbal description . . . instead of a script. "We will be conducting a new play that people are going to rave about: it will be a musical comedy, set in contemporary New Work, with songs sung by heavily costumed cats, with great choreography! Doesn't this sound exciting?"

Imagine the theater professional asking for more details about the upcoming play . . . and hearing the Director say, "I just told you!" followed by an impatient repeat of the earlier description.

It is the role of the leader to ensure that there is a clear direction for any desired organizational change. Over the years, we have seen successful changes that have started with a design that came from an autocratic decree to a heavily participative process involving literally hundreds of people in the organization and its marketplace. Our favorite approach, and the one we think works best, uses a mixture of participation from those organization members who can see the future . . . and decisive leadership who is willing to cut off debate at some point and make a call. "Making a call" means stating for the record the direction of the desired change. An example of the desired direction is Bell Helicopter's vision of "having the world's most reliable helicopters and the world's most responsive service to its customers." After days of meetings discussing vision and strategy alternatives, the Bell CEO stopped the debate and "made the call."

Detail the Vision for Organizational Change

It is one thing to have the direction of organizational change in mind; it is another to give that direction a voice or a presence that organization members can grasp. In the detailing step, we want to paint a richly-textured picture of how the organization will operate after the desired change.

Some of the best Visions we have seen for organizational change are considerably longer and more detailed than a few short bullet points on a half sheet of paper. One of our long-time clients was COO of a large financial organization. He made one pass at articulating his vision for the year 2017 for the firm's sales network made of some 4,000 offices. His first pass was documented using the traditional approach of six quick bullet points on one page.

The COO and his direct reports conducted a half-day session with the next twenty or so managers to explain the vision . . . using the six bullet points as the primary explanation tool. As the sessions were going along, the COO leaned over to me and said, "I can tell that our message is not getting across. What do we do?"

The COO finished that session and went back to the drawing board . . . or in his case, the PC. Over the next week, he turned the bullet point vision into a 20+ page short story that illustrated in great detail the bullet points. His story was about a prospective customer who tried to do business with the financial organization in the year 2017. The COO detailed what the prospective customer did, how the organization responded, how actual people in the organization worked with the customer . . . what they said and exactly what they did. After the short story was complete, the COO gave it to the same twenty or so managers who had been in the first explanation session. Their response was simple and straight forward: "Now we get it. Now we understand what the bullet points meant and how the vision could work!"

Test the Vision for Organizational Change

We don't know if we have a vision statement that can guide organizational change unless we test it with organization members. What will our organization look like once first-rate customer service has been implemented? We want the vision message tested with representatives of the organization to ensure that it is understandable, valid, complete, possible, resourceable, and compelling.

One of our clients recently finished such a test with his organization. The President of this international company and some twenty members of his organization had just completed the design and detailing of their vision for the future. They wanted to gauge employee reaction to the wording of the vision before they went into organization-wide communication.

About twenty employees representing both the headquarters and the field organizations were brought together for a two-hour session in which the President and his management team walked the group through the vision of the future. The President and his team found out that their vision and direction for the future were clear and compelling; but they also found out that the growth objectives in the vision were too numerous and overwhelming. Is that all, you say? Yep, it's that simple. The unfortunate fact of the matter is that many organizations launch a full-scale change effort without a simple vision test like the one recently used by our client!

PPI Example 1A:
Constructing the detailed vision of Perfect Service

The CEO convened his team of direct reports and their direct reports and held a "shut-in until they had sorted thru where PPI was and why they were there. They realized that the only key to their success would be to differentiate themselves in customer service. (The competitors were just too large and had too many economics of scale for PPI to become anywhere close to being the low-cost producer). (NOTE: This "mother of all shut-ins" lasted for three consecutive weeks, eight to five, with no phones and no pagers. The team ran the business after 5pm and on weekends!)

In the shut-in they decided on the following:

- We see the company holding our current level of profitability with some cost reductions and careful management of resources.

- We see the company being the number one in customer satisfaction by giving "Perfect Service" (0% late deliveries, 0% complaints, 0% incorrect invoices).

- We see the company with a revolving set of task teams working on a continuous series of improvements that are regularly measured by outside auditors and examiners.

- We see the company working smoothly within the Run-the-Business/Change-the-Business model, setting aggressive goals for both RTB and CTB . . . and looking at measurements of goal achievement side-by-side.

CEO: We defined a long-term sustainable vision from a clean sheet of paper: "To achieve long-term superior returns on capital employed by becoming the 'Supplier of Choice' for key customers in the plastics market." We defined Critical Success Factors (CSFs) to achieve focus and alignment on our annual Change-the-Business (CTB) targets. CSFs were: Competitiveness (Costs); Customer satisfaction (Revenue) and Continuous Improvement (i.e., of internal business processes, e.g., order to cash [OTC]).[21]

---

[21] We will use "Perfect Service" as short for the PPI vision even though the full vision contained other elements.

The CEO had a clear vision of the change process he wanted PPI to adopt. He envisioned Run-the-Business/Change-the-Business Management Systems with specific change goals and projects each year until the vision for the future was achieved. He envisioned himself and his executive team as the primary actors in the CTB Management System rather than staff and low-level task forces making attempts to lead change.

Detailing the Vision of the Management of Change (OPM)

Senior management must paint a picture of how the organization will be managing organizational changes in the future (i.e., with OPM). An explanation of the vision could easily start with the use of the ideas in the first half of Chapter One of this book so that the organization understands Run-the-Business/Change-the-Business. The detailed OPM vision could go forward to describe Change-the-Business as an orderly and disciplined process . . . like the organization's Run-the-Business operation.

The detailed vision of how to manage change might include a story that tells how the organization might manage an organizational change some two years in the future. The OPM story could describe:

1. Meetings between Marketing Department members and senior managers about a new market challenge that is just emerging

2. Broad discussions in the company led by executives and Marketing Department members about how to meet and profit from that challenge

3. A meeting of top management and selected others to identify a vision of how the company would need to be operating in the future to take advantage of the challenge

4. Further discussions of how to turn the vision into broad actions or strategies that must be implementing to enable the vision

5. Follow-on discussions that add financial, human resources, and information technology leaders to sort through the broad actions and to select and order the portfolio of actions the company would need to undertake in the next 12 months

6. Analysis of the portfolio of needed actions to sort actions into logical groups or Programs . . . and discussion of the Executive Team to select one or more Program Managers

7. Discussions between the Executive Team and Program Managers to select discrete projects and Project Managers to produce the unique deliverables needed for the change to the way of doing business that would meet the market challenge

8. Collaborations between Program and Project Managers to select, charter, and train project teams

9. Project teams focused on working their deliverables under the direction of Program Managers who ensure that projects support each other as needed, don't collide with and impede others

10. Change Engineers working with the line organizations to get them ready to incorporate the deliverables (new processes, procedures, tools, etc.) that are produced by the change projects

11. Change-over of the Run-the-Business organization to the new way of doing business so that the change vision would be achieved.

Requirement 1B: Constructing the case for change, the partner to the vision

> *Mind-Clearing Example—Imagine questions from the cast to the Director: Why are we changing to a new play? Aren't we still getting good reviews and making good money?*
>
> *The Director says, "We are making great money, but the producer has so much money that our play is barely noticeable to him. So . . . his spouse says the play is getting boring, so . . . we are changing the play!"*

Organization members seem to respond better to organizational change when they understand why the change is necessary and/or desirable. The case for organizational change is, therefore, a rational explanation of the need to change . . . put in terms of value to organization members. There are several stakeholders (persons or entities that have something "at stake" with the organization) involved with every organization. But one stakeholder is more critical than others for the change. An organizational change must be made by the organization's members . . . and they are the ones who need to see both the wisdom and the personal consequences of the change if they are to be vitally involved in making that change happen. The critical question to be answered is: Do stakeholders understand the importance and the need for OPM?

The case for change can be derived from another kind of future vision for the organization . . . the future the organization and its employees will face if changes are not made in the way it is doing business. Can we be effective in the absence of OPM in our company? This method for deriving the case for change comes from a simple visioning process to predict the organization's vitality and health level if it continues to operate into the future in just the way it does now.

Develop the case for change

It is the role of the leader to ensure that there is a clear and compelling case for any desired organizational change. The method the leader uses to identify the case for change is largely immaterial. Any attempt to change an organization is a big undertaking with high stakes . . . an undertaking that always has real risks to the continued healthy operation of the organization, to uninterrupted service to customers, to the earnings of the investors, and to the total working environment of the employees. If the case for change is not strong, change will be very unlikely to happen as the leader wants it to. What is the cost of not having an effective OPM infrastructure in place? Are we satisfied with our track record for change projects?

The case for change drives simple bottom line statements for the organization's three stakeholders. If we don't change the way we do business:

- Investors well not be satisfied with our performance
- Customers will not want to keep up a business relationship with us because of our level of performance.
- Employees will not be satisfied with their security or their work environment.

If a compelling case for change cannot be honestly and realistically made, the organization would be better off without the change!

Test the case for Organizational Change

We don't know if we have a case for change that will work unless we test it with the members of the organization. We want to see if people can identify with personal consequences for themselves as we unfold the case for change.

If test employees don't identify undesirable personal consequences for them, you may not have a case for change that will serve you well. Make your case or abandon your plans to make a change!

OPM NOTE 1B

There are few lines that are as compelling as the ones from the CEO who says: "This company has not done a good job of making changes in the past. Now we have big changes in front of us, and we will do a better job of managing change. Now here is the way we are going to manage change, starting now."

It is likely that any company that is attempting to implement OPM has not had a great record of managing change. So a case for using OPM can frequently be made by "very carefully" calling attention to previous change attempts that had not gone so well. The obvious problem with this approach is that old wounds may be opened and bitter feelings rekindled.

Some may build a case for change to OPM by describing what the consequences to the company and its workforce might be if a more effective and efficient method of change (like OPM) is not implemented. If the company does not do a better job of managing change, we will:

- *Slip further behind competitors*
- *Become lost in a jumble of change task forces and committees*
- *Waste time, resources, and our energy*
- *Frustrate and wear ourselves out as we have done before.*

Requirement 1C: Ensure management understanding and commitment

Mind-Clearing Example—Imagine a Director who is communicating the new play to the bit actors and stage hands while the lead actors and the stage manager look on . . . and shake their heads in disagreement with everything the Director says.

Imagine the musicians hearing the Director with one ear while hearing with the other ear the Conductor mumble to those around him, "Really dumb idea! This musical score is going to be a joke!"

Organization members react to their bosses. Period. If you want to make an organization change, you better get all the managers in the organization signed up and ready to play . . . or the change is not likely to work. It is critical for all managers to:

- Understand the vision and case for organizational change,
- Understand leadership's expectations that all managers be a part of leading/managing the change,
- Be totally committed to making the change happen.

Many leaders would think that this is a tall order . . . and it may be in some organizations. But our advice is simple, do not attempt a change without the managers on board. If the change is required for business success, you can either get all your mangers on board . . . or change to managers who will be on board!

We have seen more change efforts scuttled by uncommitted managers than by any other problem. Managers who are not committed to the change are a clear mixed signal to employees. If top management signals a change but other managers don't go along with it, the employees are in a box . . . and they will usually resolve their mixed feelings by taking the position of the manager who is closest to them on the organization chart (i.e., the manager who will sign their performance evaluation). All organization members are responsible to somebody in the organizational hierarchy . . . that's what they figure out after only a few days on the job. It is totally nonsensical to ask an organization member to put her job in jeopardy by taking up a change that her boss doesn't agree with!

A change scuttled by uncommitted managers? Whose fault is that? The fault can only lie at the feet of top management who have not ensured that their management team has gotten the change message. "We are making a change. We have gathered significant, high quality input from organization members at all levels. We have talked it through as a management team, and we are ready to change the way we are doing business. Either you step forward with the change or go immediately to your direct supervisor and either ask for a transfer or tender your resignation."

It has always struck us as very interesting that organizations go through tough, gut-wrenching deliberations to face the reality of their marketplace and decide that they must change . . . and then serve up that change to the organization as though the change were optional! We don't mean that managers stand in front of employees and use the word "optional" with regard to change . . . they don't. But they do talk about the change in such "iffy" and half-hearted tones that employee wind up feeling the change is optional. Sometimes managers go out of their way to be sensitive to employee feelings, and ask employees about the change rather than announcing that, after thoughtful problem solving, the change will occur.

If the organization needs to change for prosperity or survival sake, then the change is not optional! Announce the change, don't ask the organization what they want to do. If the change is required for organizational prosperity or survival reasons, there is no way out . . . the organization must change and the people associated with that organization must change the way they perform their roles. Organization members always have the option of going along with the change or not . . . translated to mean "staying in the organization and cooperating in the change or leaving the organization."

When we receive harsh criticism about our "change is not an option" message, we ask, "Should the director of a new play allow key players to stay in the cast and act the old play on one part of the stage while the rest of the actors performs the new play?"

Conducting management work-through sessions

Getting management on board for a change is much easier if what we call work-through sessions are conducted with all managers who have a part or stake in the change. Management work-through has two critical steps: meeting with groups of managers followed by one-on-one sit-down sessions between each manager and his boss.

The purpose of the group sessions is to allow managers to:

- Absorb the idea of the change
- Work through the ramifications of the change for themselves and their troops.

The sessions are also the opportunity to get management "in the know" before their employees get introduced to the change. Managers must know about the change first . . . lest their authority and credibility be undercut with their employees . . . who need to know and feel that their boss is part of the leadership structure of the company.

Management work-through sessions are simply meetings of groups of managers with the leaders of the company to discuss the impending change. The key idea is to give the managers the opportunity to hear about the impending change first hand, to ask questions about the change, and even to challenge the change . . . both from a rational and emotional point of view. After all, we pay managers to question and challenge ideas to ensure their validity before action, don't we? So why not allow that challenge here? In many such sessions we have seen great ideas be developed that add to the design of the vision and the case for change.

We have also seen the effect of different learning styles in such discussions. With certain adult learners, the need to question and criticize something, to state "that will never work" and so forth, is necessary for hearing and understanding. The leader's role is to keep his cool during the discussions and trust that most managers will both understand the impending change and recognize that their job is to make that change happen.

Now before we get into the detailed methods for a work-through session, let's remember where we are in the organizational change process. We have already developed and tested our vision for organizational change and the case for change. Several of the managers we are about to address may have already been involved in developing either the vision or the case for change. In either case, the change has been decided, and there is no turning back.

During the conduct of the work-through sessions, it is critical for the leader of the group session to lead the change in word and deed. We mean the following:

1. **The job is to change:** The change leader should have a presence and tone that says, "We are making this change happen because it is our job. As your CEO, I am the leader of the change, and it will happen on time, on target, and on budget." The leader, like an actor, must be serious and committed to the change.

2. **Change is not an option:** The leader should clearly convey that the change is not optional. The challenge is to implement that change efficiently.

3. **All Managers make change happen:** The leader should clearly convey her expectations that all the mangers in the firm will be on board and help with the implementation of the change.

4. **Change for the better:** The leader should convey her excitement about the opportunity to change the organization for the better and her confidence that the change will be good for the organization and its employees.

5. **Management teamwork for change:** The leader should convey the message that the change will be done in an orderly, planned way with each member of the management team doing his/her part to make the change happen.
6. **Change will be worth it:** The leader should acknowledge the extra work and the difficulty that comes with organizational change and clearly state her conviction that the organization and employees will be in a better place after the change has been completed and the new way of doing business produces the desired results.

We cannot over-emphasize the importance of leadership presence during this critical step in change. These management work-through sessions are critical for the organizational change . . . and the leader must look and be serious and committed or the sessions will move the change back and not forward!

Testing management to ensure they are on board

Management work-through is not complete until we have ensured that all of our managers are on board with the change. The only way to ensure understanding of the impending change and willingness to be a part of leading the organization through it is to conduct a face-to-face, one-on-one meeting with each manager in the organization. In that meeting the leader hears and sees for herself that the manager does understand both the vision and the case for change and will be "ready, willing and able" to work in the new way of doing business.

The interviewing manager might ask questions such as:

- What do you think the most important part of the change will be for your unit?
- How do you plan to explain the case for change to your team?

The contents of the questions to be asked are not that important. What is important is that the leader interacts long enough with the manager around the change subject to reassure herself that the manager has understood the vision and case for change and is "on board."

After ensuring understanding, the leader must move on to reassure herself that the manager is willing to support the change. (Remember that we said the change is not optional for the organization. That doesn't mean that all organization members will be willing to go along with it). The best way to deal with the "readiness to support" issue is simply to ask the manager point blank: "Can I count on you? Are you ready to support me to make this change happen on target, on time, and on budget?" Since many employees would be reluctant to give any answer other than "yes," the leader should hold out an honest offer to allow the manager to consider the questions and come see the leader before the week is over. The leader might say, "If I have not heard from you to the contrary by the end of business this week, I will assume you are NOT on board."

Now get this, the leader closes the one-on-one meeting with the manager with our cultural signal of business agreement . . . the handshake. This handshake clearly symbolizes a business agreement and is the single most compelling action the leader can take with a manager. The handshake indicates that the manager understands the impending change and the leader's expectation that the manager will be involved in implementing it . . . as well as the manager's full commitment to the new way of doing business.

For organizations with more than one level of management between the CEO and the employees, management work-through sessions will need to be conducted a layer of management at a time until the entire management chain of command has been brought to a common level of understanding and willingness to implement.

We do not want to put several layers of management in the same room at the same time for work-through sessions for a key reason. We want to maintain the authority of the chain of command and the credibility of each manager by having her work through the change message before her direct reports. We want her to feel free to question and even argue about the upcoming change and get on board with it before she works the change with her direct reports. If a manager and her direct reports hear about a change at the same time, the direct reports will wonder why their boss wasn't in on or privy to the leadership decision about change.

Even though the CEO and his executive team had already worked with each other and their next level of managers, the CEO felt that one-on-one's were needed between executives and their direct reports to ensure understanding of the Perfect Service vision.

The CEO started the ball rolling by meeting one-on-one with each of his direct reports. The CEO's meetings went well, with each executive excited about the road ahead and committed to both Run-the-Business and Change-the Business. The CEO was very pleased as he went into his last two one-on-one meetings with executive team members. These two managers had been tough to schedule . . . what with delays and cancelations.

In each of the meetings with the last two of his direct reports, the CEO sensed some softness about acceptance of the CTB requirement. He was concerned enough to participate in the one-on-one meetings that those two executives had with their direct reports. (Yes, we know. That made the meetings two-on-one!)

OPM NOTE 1C

Ensuring management understanding of OPM is not as easy and straight forward as one might think. While the Boss-to-Managers conversation about the vision of Perfect Service usually progresses quite smoothly, the same is not true for OPM. We have found, however, that the use of the Run-the-Business/Change-the-Business approach is a good foundation for the discussion.

As you read in the case above, two senior executives were not only skeptical about "Perfect Service," they were literally closed to the idea of Managers being responsible for both Running and Changing-the-Business. Their reaction is not uncommon, as *years and years of only Running-the-Business can develop strong boundaries around the ideas of what a manager should and should not do. As a further complication, some managers who can skillfully manage their Run-the-Business assignment discover that leading or participating in change initiatives is not easy for them to do at all. Run-the-Business thinking and Change-the-Business thinking are very different and some folks don't seem to be wired to do both well.*

To make the PPI long story short, after a few weeks, the CEO made the two reluctant executives "an offer they could not refuse," and they left the company shortly thereafter.

Requirement 1D: Communicating the vision the right way

Mind-Clearing Example—Imagine a Director who is trying to communicate the new play to a theater company with an opener like this, "OK folks, I'm only going to tell you the contents of this play one time . . ."

Or imagine that Director giving out only one copy of the script for the entire theater company. Better yet, imagine the Director who says, "I don't want to bore you with all the details of the script, so here is a memo summarizing the key themes in the play."

Communicating the vision and case for organization change the right way is a simple idea that is tough to execute. The right way means to communicate the message so that every member of the organization that is changing gets to hear the message enough times and in enough ways to be able to understand what they need to do. Our experience is that most leaders start the communication process with good intentions, but they typically do not follow through with the detailed steps that are needed. Successful organizational change depends on a systematic and redundant approach to communicating change.

Plan for communicating change

Communicating a new play to a theater company of two dozen can be a relatively simple exercise of calling one all-hands meeting and talking everyone through the script, encouraging them to take notes in their individual copies of the script and to ask questions until they felt comfortable. But for an organization of 14,000 employees spread over 30 countries, communication is not quite so easy.

For a change situation involving a large workforce, a comprehensive communication program is needed. The communication plan must identify the specific populations among the employees, the specific location of those employees, their work shifts/schedules, the languages and/or cultures, the communication devices that are available, and the overall timetable for the impending change. The bottom line requirement for the communication plan is that it be a detailed solution to the problem of getting each person the information he needs, when he needs it, to have him be involved in a change that occurs on target, on time, and on budget. OPM will impact all project teams and support organizations in addition to the PMO, such as Quality Assurance, Finance, Configuration Management, among a few. It is important for everyone to understand when they will be brought into the implementation picture.

Use all available communication devices

Most companies already have a variety of communication devices that they use in their day-to-day businesses. However, the primary communication device is the chain of command . . . the direct linkage between managers and every member of the organization. This primary channel must be used to communicate about organizational change or the members of the organization will not see the impending change as having anything important to do with them. Other communication devices, like electronic bulletin boards, newsletters, training classes, safety meetings, and staff meetings are already standard and accepted means of communication. These other devices should be used to accompany and/or reinforce the chain of command message . . . but they can never substitute for it!

We know that it is not popular in some circles to even mention a phrase from the past . . . like "chain of command" . . . but the truth is, every organization has one, and the employees in every organization respond to it. This chain of command linkage between boss and organization member is a primary mechanical connection that makes up a part of the structure of any organization. Organizations cannot be changed on target, on time and on budget without using the chain of command linkage. Imagine a theater company without a Director trying to get a new play ready and onto the stage in perfect timing for opening night.

An Enterprise PMO, as it prepares for the implementation of any organizational change, will have the necessary tools to enable massive communication to the organization.

Use proven communication principles

There are four principles that we believe are required for effective communication about impending organizational change. (See the appendix for more details on principles)

1. **Two-way communication**—that allows organization members to ask questions and give feedback about the change—is required for a high comprehension level.
2. **All communication bases** should be used including visual, aural and emotional messages.
3. **Repetition** will be required to convey a change message to the entire organization.
4. **Rich, face-to-face communication** will be required for organization members to communicate at maximum levels of effectiveness about the change.

Work the communication plan to desired results

Plan your work and work your plan. In the context of communicating change, working your plan is important . . . and working your plan well, crisply, and in a well-organized way can take you a long way toward successful organizational change.

We have seen great damage done to change efforts by managers who are unprepared to communicate change. We can hardly expect an organization to change on target, on time and on budget if the organization's managers cannot communicate about the impending change on target, on time, and on budget! Imagine what it says to an organization when its managers start the change communication meeting late, without needed materials, with unfocused projectors, poorly prepared slides, and unrehearsed remarks!

Leaders have not mastered change until they can communicate about organizational change with the same effectiveness and efficiency they have in the way they communicate routine changes in production runs, part numbers, sales prices, policies, priorities, or accreditation requirements.

PPI Example 1D: Communicating the Vision the Right Way

PPI did not use the "single grand round of communication" approach. Rather they used a variety of methods to communicate PPI industry position and intentions for Perfect Service. The CEO divided communication responsibility into three parts. He said, "I will be responsible to make sure the content of the communication is correct and complete. You, management team, will be responsible to roll the message down in your organizations, and, last but not least, you, Mr. Director of Quality, will be responsible for coming up with any communications vehicles or events. Just tell me when I need to play a 'face' part."

For the first year of the change, PPI used a number of different ways to communicate to their entire organization including:

- *"Vision communication" as the start of meetings and training program (right after the required safety briefing)*

- Vision inclusion in everything from job descriptions to the bi-monthly company newsletter
- Performance evaluations
- Annual employee meetings
- Shift meetings during each of the three shifts.

OPM NOTE 1D

CEO: *"This year we will be doing two things at once. We will work every day to satisfy our customers and to make our annual profit numbers. In addition we will be taking steps in three critical projects that will improve both our customer satisfaction scores and our profit numbers for next year. The three critical projects are Project one led by John Doe, Project Two led by Jane Dow . . .*

"Folks, the world has changed, and we will need to change in order to continue to improve our position. As of today, every one of us must Run-the-Business and Change-the-Business every day or we won't fit into today's or tomorrow's world of work."

What is the best way to communicate CTB and OPM? *The only communication of an OPM implementation that will be effective is for the CEO (and the E Team) to use the chain-of-command to formally announce OPM and then to talk about OPM at every single opportunity they have with the workforce.*

Despite the best intentions of other managers and staff professionals, their announcement of OPM intentions (instead of the CEO) will automatically send a message of "just another staff maneuver . . . and, obviously, the CEO and the E-Team don't care about it."

The CEO must "back" (stand up for) OPM . . . or OPM will never be "Real!"

Requirement 1E: Ensure employee translation of the vision

> *Mind-Clearing Example—Imagine a Director who is handing out scripts for the new play. When an actor asks, what is my role in the new play, the Director simply responds, "Oh, I don't know. Just read the whole thing, and we'll work all that out later." Or worse yet, imagine the Director saying, "I haven't even thought about you in the context of the new play. But just give it a read anyway."*

Organization members are not ready to begin an organizational change until they can personally relate to it. The purpose of personal application sessions is to bring all employees affected by the impending change to a competent level of comprehension and to ensure that they are on board for the change. Personal application sessions are very similar to the manager work-through sessions we described earlier, but obviously conducted between supervisor and working-level employee.

Every manager whose department or unit is affected by the change must conduct personal application sessions with her workers. Employee translation includes a meeting of all employees reporting to a given manager followed by a face-to-face, one-on-one session between manager and each employee. During the conduct of the group personal application sessions, the manager must lead the change with the same serious and committed tone and attitude we identified earlier for the leaders of management work-through sessions.

> *PPI Example 1E: Ensure Employee Translation of the Vision*
>
> *The PPI workforce could sense the new boss before they heard him speak. Their managers were up and busy, then there was the three-week absence of the managers who only showed up after five and on weekends. News of coming change and its nature was carried and transmitted by the managers in management meetings and in general workforce meetings.*
>
> *After the management work-through sessions had been completed, the executive team asked their direct reports to*

cascade the Perfect Service vision announcement and discussion of the change down through their departments, down to one-on-one translation sessions with each member of the workforce. The managers were asked to emphasize and discuss:

- The Run-the-Business/Change-the-Business change and how employees would be expected to play a part in both Running and Changing the business.
- The current business position of the company compared to competitors
- The PPI Vision that included the special emphasis on "perfect service"
- How the change would likely impact the employees in terms of working conditions, changes in his or her individual job, training, and compensation.

The employees were engaged in the conversation, encouraged to ask questions, and to give their opinions and their concerns. The managers closed their meetings with promise to meet again one-on-one before any changes were put into effect (see Requirement 4B in Chapter Seven).

OPM NOTE 1E

It should not be necessary to sit down with every employee in the company to ensure translation of the CTB/OPM message. The workforce will have heard the message that everyone is responsible for both running and changing the business in step 1D: Communicating the Vision the Right Way.

But for those members of the workforce who have permanent CTB/OPM assignments, employee translation sessions are a must. These sessions should be led by the CEO and/or the Director of the PMO.

And in conclusion . . .

Just as a theater company needs a script to understand the new play they are to perform, organization members need a vision to understand the company the leadership wants them to be in the future. Requirement One calls for leaders to construct and fully communicate a clear, detailed vision of the organization as they intend for it to be in the future. If the employees of an organization are going to be asked to change, they need to know what that change will look like. And they need as much information about that change as they can get so that they can begin to integrate that picture of the future into their current way of thinking.

The vision we need to construct can either be for the entire organization undergoing change (e.g., a meter company becoming a smart meter company) or the vision can be for one of the change projects that will lead to the change vision (e.g., building a microwave engineering function that would enable the vision of smart meters.)

For OPM, our vision should be one of having critical change projects continuously aligned with our company strategies. Because of OPM, only the right change projects would be worked on and completed on time and on budget. These projects would be managed by certified project managers and controlled by the Enterprise PMO, also responsible for communicating status to all stakeholders on a regular basis.

A vision for change is certainly critical. A vision is necessary, but not sufficient for change. A vision, regardless of how well-communicated is not enough to lead a successful organizational change. The other moving parts described in later chapters will tell the rest of the story. When taken together, vision and the other moving parts will be sufficient for an organizational change . . . on target, on time, and on budget.

Chapter Five

Altering Work Processes and Procedures

Mind-Clearing Example—Imagine a Director who assumes that everything that needs to be worked out about the actors' performance is in the script. "It is all written right there . . . and you can probably do some of the stuff that was in the last play."

Imagine not working out detailed game plans for starting and stopping the music, when curtains are to open and close, when scenery and backdrops are to be changed, when actors enter and leave the stage, etc. etc.

Implementation of a vision cannot occur until existing work processes and procedures are physically modified to enable a new way of doing business. Implementation cannot occur until the machinery of the workflow is successfully altered and tested. In this chapter we will focus on changing the physical steps the organization will need to use in the new way of doing business. Failing to alter work processes and still expecting change is akin to expecting the performance of a new play from a theater company whose actors are acting in their old parts.

OPM will require many new processes, which will include the annual development and/or revision of a company vision, the implementation of portfolio and program management processes, as well as the adoption of leading-edge project management processes. Specific processes for developing a company's core products will also be required, as each product development process will need to be governed by a detailed project management methodology, quality assurance steps, configuration management tasks, etc.

Identify and dispel deadly assumptions that will disable the alteration of processes

The step of altering work processes to enable the change vision is perhaps the most important step to get right. Process steps take inputs and turn them into outputs, and without processes there would be no organizational outcomes. When transitioning an organization to a new way of doing business, very careful attention must be paid to the validity of the process steps that will make up the new way of doing business.

However, in the day-to-day running of a business, process steps are practically invisible as employees complete work steps they have been completing for some time. In many cases, employees are blind to the reasons or thinking behind the steps they complete, not having had to develop those steps through design or trial and error. The tendency of many managers, therefore, is to assume that people know the process steps and if changes are needed, employees will work them out as they go along toward the new way of doing business. But such is not the case as many who have left processes to meander toward the future have found out.

Step	Change-Blocking Assumption	Disabling Behavior	Proven Consequences
Requirement Two: Alteration of Process(es) and Procedures	If people understand the direction of change, they will start using the right processes automatically.	Downplaying process analysis; depending on individuals to work through processes themselves.	• Inconsistent performance • Sub-optimized improvement • Anxiety

Change leaders can spot the likely presence of deadly assumptions about work processes through conversations heard about what needs to be done. Hearing the suggestion "we don't need all this process mapping stuff; our people will shift to new processes automatically as we go along" calls for the change leader to surface such deadly assumptions and to dispel them in any way possible, starting with the proven consequences in the table above.

Take these action steps to Complete Requirement Two: Altering work processes

Now we are on to the hard work of altering work processes using the following five steps. Skip one of the steps below and expect the change to a new way of doing business to derail.

Action steps to transition work processes

- 2A: Identify work process alterations needed for the change
- 2B: Alter and test work processes critical for the change
- 2C: Alter process measures, goals, and objectives to match processes
- 2D: Alter and test work procedures for altered processes
- 2E: Eliminate old measures, goals, objectives and procedures

---

Requirement 2A: Identify the process alterations needed for change

Mind-Clearing Example—Imagine a Director who has not worked through in her mind exactly what she wants the actors to do in their newly assigned roles.

Imagine she knows that she wants to depict young men in the streets committed to revolution . . . but she has not yet visualized or communicated the "manning of the barricades" on stage. Or imagine the lunatic Director who transitions the company to a new play but who allows the actors to repeat the scenes from the previous play!

If a theater company doesn't change what happens on stage, the audience will swear that the play has not changed . . . despite the new name on the marquee. If the day-in and day-out steps organization members take as they go about their work do not change, then the organization has not changed . . . despite any words, slogans, or banners to the contrary.

I can imagine a reader inexperienced in the street-fighting of organizational change wondering why we are making such "no brainer" assertions. After watching organizational change for thirty years, we will tell you that it is common place for an organization's top management to come up with a statement of a new vision, and still allow the organization to conduct day-to-day operations in essentially the same way they had been working for the last five years . . . leaving the optimists among the workforce to wait for a miracle and the cynical to wait for the change effort to be allowed to slowly fade away.

Change requires work process alterations

By virtue of the mechanical nature of organizations, every organizational change requires at least one change in work process. Regardless of the kind of organizational change or the stimulus for organizational change, work process alterations will be required.

o   If an organization decides to change its business strategy (e.g., to become the low-cost service provider in its market segment), many, if not all, of the organization's service delivery processes will need to change to take out costly non-value adding steps or to alter the sequence of those steps. In addition, the organization's marketing processes would need to be altered to add the steps and promotional materials that will reflect a more flexible pricing structure that will make the company a better value than the competition.

o   If an organization decides to install a new inventory control system to expedite manufacturing, work process changes will be involved. Work steps will need to change in order to set-up the new software, and processes and procedures will need to change to reflect the operating guidelines of the software.

o If an organization decides to make a change in its culture (e.g., with culture defined as "the way we do things around here"), several process changes will need to be made to require organization members to approach their jobs differently. If, for example, the desired cultural change is to become more attentive to customers, changes will probably need to be made in the work steps and mindsets used in customer service such as informing customers what to expect, expressing concern about their situation, and moving rapidly to fix the customer's problem.

o It will be impossible to adopt OPM effectively in the absence of appropriate change management and a significant change in the processes used for managing projects, programs, and portfolios and in the processes used to ensure that these are constantly aligned with the organization's business strategies. The Enterprise PMO will have to manage these process changes, which are definitely not trivial.

Start with an Inventory of Work Processes

The first step in identifying needed work process alterations is to systematically review the organization's current work processes and visualize any alterations that will be needed, given the vision of a new way of doing business. We have found it easier to identify work processes that will be affected by an impending change by looking through the organization's existing inventory of work processes.

In case the organization does not have a work process inventory—and many organizations do not—we have found the following list of generic processes to be a good starter for discussion as organization members look for processes that might need to be altered.

While the names that organizations use for their own work processes vary greatly, almost all organizations need to use the following core work processes in order to stay in business:

- Identify groups of customers where the organization's services might be needed
- Develop services that can be competitively sold in those customer markets
- Make sales to specific customers and finalize terms and contracts
- Provide services (quality, satisfaction, outcomes) that fulfill the customers' orders
- Provide support to customers after initial service delivery
- Invoice customers for services rendered . . . and receive and record payments

Obviously there are many sub-processes that make up each of these core processes. For example, under the "get contracts" (make sales) work process, there will be sub-processes to identify prospects, research needs of those prospects, schedule negotiation calls, conduct marketing engagements, etc.

In searching for processes that might need to be altered, be aware that such a process could be almost anywhere in the organization. In addition to the core work processes cited above, organizations also have processes that manage the performance of the business as a whole (e.g., executive decision making processes), business processes (e.g., annual budgeting), and employees performance (e.g., the performance appraisal system). Yes, it can be like an Easter egg hunt to find and target processes that need to be altered. Someone also said that it was a bit like shooting pool . . . since altering one process might start a ripple effect of needed alterations in other work processes.

There is nothing elegant about the process inventory work described above. Inventorying is a comprehensive mechanical exercise designed to be thorough and comprehensive . . . not elegant. While some organization members describe the process of identifying needed alterations as fun, others see it as pure drudgery. Regardless of the attitude, fun or no fun, this step must be done and done well. Many changes have gone awry because the change planners did not take the time to comprehensively review all of their organization's work processes and specifically identify the alteration work needed for the change to a new way of doing business.

PPI Example 2A: Identify the process alterations needed for change

CEO: "We started development of our first list of needed process changes by end-to-end process mapping. We convened our senior team (myself and two levels of direct reports) for three weeks of full-time work from 8-5 (no phone calls, no lunches out) until we got it done. We ran the daily business after 5 p.m. and on Saturdays and Sundays during the three-week period."

Three of the more than two dozen processes that were identified for improvement of customer satisfaction were in:

1. *Accuracy and timeliness in scheduling of freight cars*
2. *Completing the shipment paperwork that went to customers along with product*
3. *Re-designing the customer feedback forms and satisfaction survey*

Each work process identified for improvement was eventually assigned to a project team for analysis and problem solving.

OPM NOTE 2A

At the end of the three-week session, PPI executives were clear on the needed direction of change (Perfect Service) in the way they did business, but they were also clear on how they as the Executive Team would manage change. An inventory of processes currently used to manage change (task forces and projects had been completed during the mapping exercise. Change projects were more extensive than estimated, since project work impacts so many aspects of the organization, from initiating strategic planning to the last task needed to close a company project. Executives and their direct reports understood the work processes that would be used then (and in the future) for Change-the-Business. The summary of how they agreed to manage change is shown in their Change Management Plan below:

PPI Plan for Managing Change

1. The CEO was to be the owner of Change-the-Business for the company.

2. Early, detailed visioning would be the first critical step in the CTB/OPM method

3. During Visioning, the needed actions to reach the vision would be identified

4. Since all the needed actions could not take place at once, and since some actions would need to be completed before others, the senior team would construct the portfolio of actions that would need to be worked in sequence for the next two years.

5. Program Managers were to be appointed to manage the change work for the upcoming year. Program Managers would report directly to the CEO.

6. The Program Managers worked with the Executive Team and the Director of Quality to name and staff projects in each Program. Project Managers would be named by Program Managers with the concurrence of the Executive Team.

7. Program and Project Managers would work together to name project team members, and then to charter each team.

8. The Director of Quality and his team would be assigned to "staff the change and support Program and Project

Managers." (In today's terms, the Director of Quality would have been called the Manager of the PMO).

9. The Director of Quality, working under the CEO's directions, would arrange for training in (a) Project Management for each Project Manager and (b) training in process improvement methods for all team members. The Executive Team would take the same training as Project Teams to be in sync with their Program and Project personnel.

10. Each member of the Executive Team would be responsible for implementation of approved change project deliverables for their areas of responsibility. Each executive would have some Change Engineering support for his implementations, but the ball would officially stay in the Executive's court for complete implementation.

11. The last summary point in how change would be managed was added by the CEO as the finale of the discussion: executive compensation in the form of incentive pay would be totally contingent on each executive's Change-the-Business performance (including the success level of implementation of the approved actions and recommendations from Program Managers). (More on this step later.)

Requirement 2B: Alter and test processes critical to the change

Mind-Clearing Example—Imagine a Director who has an idea about what an actor in the new play should be doing, but who fails to work through the details of the idea with the actor.

Or imagine the Director working through the new ideas in his mind but not actually testing them with the actors on stage. When asked specifically by an actor what he should do, the Director responded, "Oh, don't worry about it; we will work that through on opening night!"

The tendency in organizational change is to talk about how the organization needs to do business differently but to not really do anything about it. That same tendency is alive and well in the area of work process alteration. The steps in the work processes that have been identified for alteration must be physically altered, not just discussed. But where does this alteration take place? It takes place first and foremost on paper (or on a software program) and second in the trenches where the organization's workers actually use the new process steps as a part of the new way of doing day-to-day work.

Draw pictures of new work processes

The key step in physically altering work processes is to draw pictures or "workflow diagrams" of the new steps, much like an architect would do, required for each work process involved by the new way of doing business. Most organizations today already have experience with process mapping and documentation. And many organizations are already using automated tools for such mapping . . . so use them! Our purpose in this book is not to describe the well-developed fields of process improvement or mapping. Our purpose is to make the point that many of the tools of process improvement, especially process mapping, should be applied in every organizational change!

We have had clients push back when we tell them that mapping process alterations is a must. Several have responded, "I thought we did all that during the last process improvement effort !" Our response is simple. We must re-map processes as a part of every organizational change . . . or there will likely be no organizational change. Altering processes remains a requirement . . . despite how detailed and tedious it might be and despite how much work has been done on work processes in the past. Imagine the theater Director who makes the following bizarre statement, "No need to think through the details of roles in the new play, we did detailed thinking for roles in the previous play!

The Enterprise PMO will be tasked to support the necessary modifications to the processes that have been identified for the new way of doing business. It will not be a simple job, but one that will require additional change engineering strategies and tasks, as these process will end up impacting virtually every employee in the organization. OPM

implementation will require prototyping efforts to ensure that projects using new or modified processes and procedures are actually efficient and effective. The Enterprise PMO will have to guide these prototyping activities to make sure things are working well. Executing two to three projects as prototypes will be key to the success of OPM implementation.

PPI Example 2B: Alter and test work processes critical to the change

PPI combined identifying impacted processes and their alteration and test. At the end of the three weeks, all core processes had been documented, some processes had been redesigned during the session, other more complex processes were listed to be assigned to projects teams for process improvement. Given the number of processes identified for improvement and the need to make something happen for customers, improvement projects were scheduled to run in series and in parallel during the first three years of the new CEO's tenure.

OPM NOTE 2B

The Director of Quality (he would likely have been called the "PMO" Manager today) was indispensable during the three solid weeks of work and thereafter when he and his staff worked with the CEO to ensure that project teams had been named to attack each improvement target and that the Projects would be managed as a Program.

The Director of Quality was Project Manager for the improvement project focused on Project Management Methods. The company had a Project Management method that was out of date, not fully documented, and for which there was no internal training program. An external subject matter expert in project management was engaged to work with the project team to improve and test what would become the company-authorized project management methodology.

Requirement 2C: Alter process measures, goals and objectives

> *Mind-Clearing Example—Imagine an actor in a comedy role being transferred to the role of the "serious villain" in a new play. Imagine the Director now saying to the actor, "Remember, your objective on the stage is to make the audience laugh."*
>
> *When questioned by the actor, the Director responds by saying, "Yes, we are changing the play, but we're not changing any goals at the individual actor level."*

We said earlier that a work process alteration would be involved in some way or another in every organizational change. There may be times when the work process steps may not need to be altered . . . if the measures, goals and objectives of the work processes are altered. We can illustrate that idea with a simple example. Imagine a marketing work process for a company that sells telephone systems to medical practices. Assume that the following steps were being used for identification of prospects in a geographical market:

- Locate a business directory for target market area
- Review listings in the directory to identify all medical practices listed
- Transfer business address/phone number and names of key managers to prospect list
- Assign market reps to call listed names to find out information about phone needs

Now let's assume that this company wants to change its strategy to include schools and city offices. All the work steps would remain essentially the same. No new process maps would need to be drawn; expanding the list of goals would be all that was required.

> **PPI Example 2C: Alter process measures, goals and objectives**
>
> *CEO: Bottom-Line business metrics were chosen. We decided to use metrics that meant something to the business world (e.g. customer satisfaction ratings, profitability margin). We wanted*

formally-defined, bullet-proof measures, not ones "we could fudge." We used objective, industry third-party services and external auditors/examiners for our metric information.

We set two kinds of hard targets that year and every year thereafter for the Run-the-Business management system:

- *Safety record*
- *Cash flow*
- *Return on capital employed, and*
- *Customer satisfaction.*

We also set stiff targets for the Change-the-Business Management System for:

- *Improving customer perception of reliability and*
- *Achieving "Perfect Service" (0% late deliveries, 0% complaints, 0% incorrect invoices).*

OPM NOTE 2C

OPM will require new measures, goals, and objectives. The Enterprise PMO will define these in concert with Senior Management. Key objectives will be to constantly maintain alignment of projects, programs, and portfolios with the organization's vision and business strategies. All implemented measures and goals will trickle down from how well we will meet this key objective. If this key objective is not met, all new measures and goals should immediately point us in that direction, if they are in any way effective.

Requirement 2D: Alter and test work procedures for altered processes

> *Mind-Clearing Example—Imagine an actor who asks for written copies of the Director's instructions and notes for playing an assigned part . . . and hearing the Director say, "Oh, I didn't have time to write down any notes; I'll give you a heads-up if I see you doing something wrong."*

Organizations use procedures to guide workers through work processes. A procedure is nothing more than a written set of instructions that describes what workers do for each step of a work process. In the organizations we have worked with over the years, we have found the widest possible range of procedures in play . . . all the way from heavily-documented, detailed, tightly-controlled work instructions for NASA flight controllers to "scrap paper notes" taped to machine tools in a manufacturing facility.

People in organizations respond to procedures, regardless of the form or rigor of the procedure. Organization members have learned the organization's way of doing work, and they know from their experience that following those ways matters. Therefore, if an organization is changing its work processes, it must also change its procedures that describe that work.

Do we really think that organizations that are trying to change would leave old procedures in play? Yep! All the time! We have seen managers describing the new ways they want to see their organizations do business while standing in the same room with procedure manuals that do not reflect those new ways! If you want your organization to change, modify existing procedures to match new processes, and publicize them. If the work process alterations in the organization have been extensive, consider having worker training classes on the new procedures.

Testing of new procedures is critical to change. The only way we will know that a new procedure will lead to the right results is to test the newly-written procedures with employees from the populations that will be expected to use them. We recommend what we call a split test to get the most useful information about a newly-written procedure. Identify the test population and split it into two test teams.

- Give Team One a thorough briefing on what you were trying to accomplish with the new procedure . . . and then let them follow the new procedure to get their work done. Watch closely to see that the procedure works.

- Give Team Two copies of the new procedures but with no explanations. Simply ask the team to read the procedure and follow the steps. Watch closely to see how this procedure works. All procedures need to be tested under the "no explanation" condition . . . because procedures will eventually find their way into the hands of people who need to use them but who have had no detailed explanation.

Make sure that the new procedures are identified with an effective or revised date. Also consider some special marking, border, or color that catches the workers' eyes and lets them know that new work instructions are in place.

Writing, modifying and testing the new procedures are the first steps. Marking those procedures as "new" is the next step. The final step with procedures is to ensure that every organization member who is to use the procedure gets copied or gets access to a copy. The procedure step is not complete until we know that each and every affected worker has the needed work instructions in hand.

Think about this: if a Director is moving his cast of twenty actors to a new play, how many copies of the new script does she need? Twenty. How many different folks need to get a copy? Twenty. How does she ensure that each actor has a copy? She hands out twenty on a personal level, or has the Stage Manager issue them and get signatures. How many signatures? Twenty. This ain't rocket science . . . but it is the thorough, detailed, work required for organizational change!

OPM NOTE 2D

Requirement 2E: Eliminate old measures, goals, objectives and procedures

Mind-Clearing Example—Imagine a Director who allows the master stage copy of the last production's script to remain open and in place right beside the master copy of the script for the new play that is currently being performed.

When asked about moving the copy from the old play, imagine the Director saying, "No, don't move it; you never know when we might need it again!"

You will be happy to know that commercial airline pilots have mastered change when it comes to new approach procedures. First of all, an approach procedure is a kind of work process that pilots use to approach an airport for landing. Each airport approach is described in a written procedure that pilots carry with them in the cockpit. Following those procedures to the letter is critical for aircraft safety.

Airports periodically change their approaches to reflect needs for better aircraft routing or safety. When they make such a change, new approach procedures are designed, dated, printed, and distributed to all pilots who will use that airport. A standard part of the physical issuance of the new approach procedures calls for the pilots to turn in their old procedures first before new ones will be issued to them! This step is designed to ensure that old, out-of-date procedures will not be used past the effective date of the new ones. Why? Because old procedures "left lying around" will be used.

Bottom line, the last critical step in altering work processes for organizational change is to take old work process maps, old procedures, old performance goals out of the work environment. How do you do that? You systematically collect them and then permanently dispose of them . . . trash them, shred them, or burn them!

In some situations, where changing to new procedures is especially vital, you might consider holding a formal ceremony to dispose of the old procedures. We have on a few occasions heard of companies that had a wake or funeral for old procedures in order to call special attention to the need to move on to the new way of doing business. While this kind of dramatic step may not be needed for organizations that have mastered change, such steps are clearly important for organizations that are just beginning to become proficient at change. I can see it now: a leader looking over the flames of an old procedure pyre into the eyes of employees mourning the loss of that last crib sheet for getting their job done, and seeing them take a deep breath to move on to the new way of doing business!

OPM NOTE 2E

And in conclusion . . .

Process steps turn inputs into desired outputs, and without processes there would be no organizational outcomes. Implementation of a new way of doing business cannot occur until existing processes and procedures are physically altered to enable that new way of doing business.

In this chapter we focused on changing the physical steps the organization uses to get its work done to ensure that a new way of operating will be possible in the future. The step of altering work processes to enable the change vision is perhaps the most important to "get right." When transitioning an organization to a new way of doing business, very careful attention must be paid to the validity of the process steps that will make up the new way of doing business. Altering processes and procedures is not enough, however. Most work processes call for the use of tools, equipment, software, etc., a vital subject to be covered in the next chapter.

Chapter Six

Altering Facilities, Equipment, and Technology (FET)

Mind-Clearing Example—Imagine a Director who fails to make arrangements to rent the theater for the new production. Or who fails to commission workmen to transfer the set and stage rigging from the configuration of the last play to the new one!

An organization cannot reach its vision of a new way of doing business unless the facilities, equipment, and technology (FET) needed to support changed work processes have been altered, tested and made available to trained employees. That is an absolute requirement. In addition, the vision will not be realized until the old FET that is not to be used after the transition has been removed from the workplace and destroyed.

Our task in this chapter is to focus on the third requirement for transitioning an organization: the physical alteration of the organization's FET. Every organizational change is likely to require new or altered FET of some kind to enable the altered work processes designed to fulfill the vision. Regardless of the kind of organizational change or the stimulus for organizational change, we work with the assumption that FET alterations will be required . . . unless proven otherwise.

We have certainly seen organizational changes that required little or no alteration in FET. As a simple example, imagine a home construction contractor who does lumber framing. Changing the place the frames are put together (e.g., at the job site or at the lumber yard) will require major alterations in work steps but require no changes in the hammers used by the framing carpenters.

On the other hand, this same framing contractor might need to change the equipment used to haul the completed, bulky frames to the job site.

Just as work process steps and procedures go together, FET and operating guidelines go together. Operating guidelines are the written instructions for proper use and operation of FET, be it a ladder, a piece of earth moving equipment or new ERP software. Failing to provide proper operating guidelines for new or altered FET is akin to expecting a new look from a play that is opening with the set and costumes left over from the last play.

Change requires alterations of Facilities, Equipment, Technology (FET)

The obvious case for altering FET comes when new FET is the organization's change focus from the beginning (e.g., "Goal: to implement Electric Medical Records—EMR"). Other cases requiring alterations of FET are driven by very different kinds of change motivations. For example:

- If a service company decides to change its business strategy to become the low cost provider, many, if not all, of the organization's delivery processes will need to change to take out costly steps or to alter the sequence of steps. Altering any parts of the work process is likely to require a different facility configuration and changed support systems.

- If an organization decides to re-engineer one of its work processes in order to achieve new efficiencies or a new level of safe operation, changes might be required in everything from guard rails to shut-off switches to business product assembly lines. As FET changes are made, corresponding changes will be needed in the written operating guidelines that support the FET changes.

- If an organization decides to make a change in its culture (e.g., with culture simply defined as "the way we do things around here"), several process changes will result as organization members begin to approach their jobs differently. If for example, the desired cultural change is to become more attentive to customers, changes will probably need to be made in the steps used in customer service departments or help desks. As alterations are made in customer service steps, modifications are likely to be required in the tools used by customer service employees, namely software applications and telecommunications equipment.

- The Enterprise PMO will have its hands full when it comes to changing facilities, equipment, and technology for OPM. From project "war rooms" to networked PCs for every project team member, from enterprise project management software to specially equipped rooms for strategic planning workshops, the Enterprise PMO will have to enable the best possible environment for successful Visioning, Portfolio, Program and Project Management and Change Engineering.

The Requirement to alter the organization's FET is both one of the "best handled" components of organizational change and one of the worst. For what we call "visible FET,"—physical plant, piping, and machine tools—alterations are usually very well done for the transition to a new way of operating. We think this kind of change is handled so well because these technologies are easily visible . . . failure to alter this kind of FET would be easy to spot and correct.

But when the FET to be altered is not easy to see, it is frequently not handled as well. For example, alteration of software to enable changes that need to be made in work processes seems much tougher to deal with for several reasons. For example, software is usually changed by specialists in back rooms; such activity is not easy to see and, therefore, workers are unlikely to see what is going on or what is coming. Even though software changes have been announced as being underway, it is frequently a surprise when workers come in to work to find "new computer screens" associated with their job. In addition, FET that needs to be added to support core FET is often overlooked or poorly handled. For example, changing the customer service software application for a help center might be completed on target, but the new telecommunication equipment for workers using that new software may be forgotten. We are kidding. No, it happens. (Our approach for dealing with the software alteration issue is covered in a later section of this chapter.)

Identify and dispel deadly assumptions that will disable FET transition

The step of transitioning FET to enable the change vision looks straight-forward. However experience has taught that nothing about change is really a slam-dunk, one-step action. Once again we face deadly assumptions, but this time those assumptions may have a hard-driving, articulate force behind them! FET vendors frequently have mantras they repetitively deliver to your organizations during work time as well as during "lubrication time" spent with your key buyers.

Popular mantras include: "Our software really does do everything! Our stuff is THE complete solution! Once our software goes live, your problem is over, and your work is finished! Implement our solution and you and your department will be the heroes of the change initiative!"

Just imagine those sweet words whispered in your ear as you stand, glass of expensive champagne in hand, salt spray in your face, breathing crisp and clear Pacific air, on the bow of the $100M yacht that is expected to win this year's America's Cup. "Ah, this really must be great FET we are buying, and it will take care of everything!"

Step	Deadly Assumptions	Disabling Behavior	Proven Consequences
Transitioning FET	1. Once the new FET is "in," the change will be taken care of. 2. The FET (or the vendor) will do everything, just like they said 3. It's just a process change, we don't even need to look at FET.	1. Leaving the FET up to the vendor. 2. Focusing exclusively on technical implementation. Not auditing the impact of FET on processes and roles	• Frustration • Unmet expectations • Return to use of old FET • Increased apprehension about change

Change leaders can spot the likely presence of deadly assumptions about FET through conversations about what needs to be done to get FET transitioned. Hearing the suggestion to "Leave the FET up to the vendor" calls for the change leader to surface deadly assumptions and to dispel them in any way possible, starting with the proven consequences in the table above.

Take These Action Steps to Complete Requirement Three: Altering FET

Now we are on to the hard work of transitioning FET using the following five steps. Skip a step and expect expensive problems.

Action steps to transition FET

- 3A: Identify the FET alterations need for the change
- 3B: Alter and test all FET needed for the change
- 3C: Alter and test each and every FET control
- 3D: Alter or create operating guidelines for all involved FET
- 3E: Eliminate old FET and operating guidelines

Requirement 3A: Identify the FET alterations needed for change

Mind-Clearing Example—Imagine a Director who selects a new play and who commits to an opening date without planning the modifications that will be needed for the props and backdrops for staging the new play.

The FET part of transitioning an organization to a new way of operating starts with the identification of the FET that will be impacted by the transition. To have any hope of making an organization successfully change, we must know, with as much certainty as possible, the construction or alterations tasks that must be completed before the FET transition can be completed.

This step to identify needed FET alterations can be anything from a huge project in itself (if the vision includes merging with another company, for example) to a short and sweet exercise (if the change is something as simple as changing employee badges for better record keeping). We have been successful in identifying needed alterations to an organization's FET with two different approaches . . . the FET inventory approach and the process inventory approach. The FET Inventory approach is the most logical to use when the organizational change is being driven primarily by the desire for new FET such as a new MRI unit, a new production facility, or a new software application. The process inventory approach is the most logical for all other kinds of organizational changes.

Approach One: The FET Inventory approach. This approach calls for examination of each element of FET that is connected to a major FET change. For example, installation of new computer equipment might call for more cooling equipment. Installing new FET almost always starts a ripple effect of needed work on existing FET to physically accommodate the new major FET change. For example, the new imaging equipment mentioned above may require a change in the space layout or the electrical power.

Approach Two: The process inventory approach. This approach calls for examination of each work process change that is contemplated, looking for the use of FET in any process step. Use of this approach to identify needed alterations in **FET** assumes that the reason for the organizational change is something other than **major FET** driven. Many alterations in **FET** are needed because the organization starts out to change its strategy, work processes, or the behavior and performance of its employees. For example, what if a hospital strategy is to distinguish the patient experience by providing on-demand room service to their patients? This strategy would require retooling the kitchen to operate more like a short order restaurant, providing extra room and technology for a call center to take orders based on diet restrictions, as well as facilities close to the patient rooms for the servers to prep and deliver the meal in their formal attire.

The bottom line fact associated with the installation and lifetime value of new FET is very simple. It is very easy and commonplace to overlook changes that are needed in existing FET to accommodate the new FET. Over the years, we have seen many organizational changes delayed because the transition to needed FET had an unexpected and un-planned ripple effect on neighboring equipment. We have seen unanticipated power drains that impact other equipment; we have seen many heating and cooling problems emerge because of new equipment operating in ways different than it was planned, and so on.

The results of a FET inventory: The kinds of alterations that could appear on a FET alteration team's list might be as follows:

- Cut pass-through window between two rooms in the quality testing lab
- Add thee more centrifuges for running smaller, faster turnaround specimen batches
- Upgrade electronic interface so that results can post on the electronic inventory record and alert the ordering unit when critical values have been exceeded.

In reality, a FET alteration team will need to repeat the inventory step at least two more times: during the installation of the newly-acquired FET and after installation is complete. Our experience over thirty years is that additional needed alterations in an organization's existing FET will continue to be found right through installation and use . . . and sometimes even months or years later!

A very special case: the alteration of software

For the purposes of this book, we will consider software to be FET . . . a very important part of FET. It is a rare organizational change these days that does not involve some information technology system. Everything that we have said so far about altering FET applies to software/systems. But many times the organization members who get involved in the alteration of FET are different when software is involved . . . that's the good news . . . and the bad news!

When we talk to information FET professionals about "altering" software, they immediately translate what we are saying into the vocabulary of their profession. Their translation becomes "application development or application sourcing." In many organizations there are Information technology (IT) professionals who specialize in "apps" or "AD." These professionals already have approaches or techniques they use to develop, modify or acquire an IT application. The first step in their usual approach is frequently called "defining requirements." Depending on the size of your organization, you may have IT professionals who specialize in defining requirements for applications development or sourcing. And therein lies both the good news and the bad news.

We have found it very difficult to intervene in a requirements definition process. Most IT professionals who do requirements definition are focused professionals using a disciplined approach to identify and record what users want their new or modified information system to do. That's the good news . . . a professional using a systematic approach can come help you with the identification of the alterations that will be needed to your software FET.

The bad news is that frequently the IT professional does not receive a really good picture of the organizational change that is driving the system alteration. This inadequate or incomplete picture can occur because the users who are interviewed by the IT professional do not have or convey a good picture of the vision . . . or because of the narrow focus of the IT professional who is only listening for technical "entering arguments" to the applications development/sourcing process. These entering arguments can be way off base because of a lack of understanding of the business and a lack of understanding of the new way of doing business being contemplated.

Our suggestion is to be relentless in your pursuit of the changes that are needed. Don't just hope that what you see next will be altered software that helps you keep your organizational change on target, on time, and on budget!

OPM NOTE 3A

The FET alterations needed to implement OPM were quickly pinpointed by the Executive Team working with the Director of Quality. They saw the need to update the out-of-date Project Management software the company had in their application inventory. They also recognized that changes would be needed to accommodate both Run-the-Business and Change-the-Business measures and results in the reporting formats used by accounting.

The FET alterations needed by PPI for moving to the Run-the-Business/Change-the-Business model looked minor at first . . . only a few software modifications to adjust reporting formats were required, but as could be expected, the modification process took an extra two weeks of work by the Information Technology Department.

Requirement 3B: Alter and test FET critical for the change

> *Mind-Clearing Example—Imagine a Stage Manager who receives the Director's list of the needed scenery changes for the new play, but who tells the puzzled stagehands "not to change anything" from the last play: "Just give it a new coat of paint," he says.*
>
> *Or imagine the Lighting Director (1) asking an electrical technician if all the spotlights had been changed to the new required colors and (2) being happy with the following answer, "Yes, kinda, I changed three of the five, and they stitch on most of the time."*

By this time the change leader should have clearly identified both the new FET needed for the impending change and the alterations that will be needed to existing FET. In this step, the change leader now needs to ensure that all the needed FET work gets done satisfactorily. In addition, he must ensure that all new and altered FET has been thoroughly tested to ensure that it operates as it needs to in order to support the Vision.

To a large degree, the change leader's success in making needed alterations in FET will be dependent on his organization's capability in two important management areas: construction management and software management. Getting needed alteration of FET (not software) will be dependent on how well the organization executes management principles as applied to the acquisition and/or construction of FET. Getting needed alterations of software FET will largely be dependent on the organization's maturity or development level in software processes.

Alteration of physical FET (i.e., "Bricks")

Consider this kind of alteration as a "construction project." For physical FET some form of the discipline of management as applied to FET acquisition must be used to have any chance of successfully installing new FET or altering existing FET (assuming that we are talking about something more than going to a hardware store and picking up a new claw hammer).

The change leaders in the organization must themselves have a "common sense construction management mindset." Some managers in today's organizations have at least some passing experience with FET or equipment purchase and/or installation (i.e., building or installing something), or they are veterans of construction projects around their homes. They may have been assigned to manage a simple construction project (re-modeling an office or buying and installing a new cabinet in the break room) or they have been around while such a project was being worked.

Change leaders can get construction management in play in FET alteration in any of three different ways . . . and their choice of a way or approach should be based on the size and complexity of the needed FET alteration.

- **Use Common Sense Management**. For small or simple purchases or installations, it may be OK to use nothing more than the common sense approach . . . but it must be done in a very disciplined way . . . with goals, budgets, and schedules and so on.

- **Engage an internal manager who is experienced in Construction Management**. Acquiring or building FET is not new for most organizations that have a history of change and/or expansion. Many organizations have qualified professionals on board who can become the acquisition manager for acquiring and/altering FET associated with organizational change.

- **For facility construction changes, if knowledge is not resident in house, engage a professional management company (or professional) from the outside**. Some organizations prefer to use outside Construction resources for large and/or complicated processes. You may be aware that there is an entire industry called "Engineering and Construction" whose mission it is to design, procure, and construct major capital projects for business.

Alteration of Software FET (i.e., "Clicks")

FET will usually be handled by the organization's Information technology Department. IT Departments in most companies are accustomed to handling such changes. But from our perspective, what counts is the IT Department's overall competence in handling software change in an orderly predictable way that will allow transition projects to be on target, on time, and on budget.

The Software Engineering Institute of Carnegie Mellon University talks about the overall capability of IT organizations to manage software processes. They talk about IT organizations that are "immature" versus those that are "mature."

"In an immature software organization, software processes are generally improvised by practitioners and their management during the course of the project. Even if a software process has been specified, it is not rigorously followed or enforced. The immature software organization is reactionary, and managers are usually focused on solving immediate crises (better known as fire-fighting). Schedules and budgets are routinely exceeded because they are not based on realistic estimates. When hard deadlines are imposed, product functionality and quality are often compromised to meet the schedule.

On the other hand, a mature software organization possesses an organization-wide ability for managing software development and maintenance processes. The software process is accurately communicated to both existing staff and new employees, and work activities are carried out according to the planned process. The processes mandated are fit for use and consistent with the way the work actually gets done. These defined processes are updated when necessary, and improvements are developed through controlled pilot-tests and/or cost benefit analyses. Roles and responsibilities within the defined process are clear throughout the project and across the organization.

"In a mature organization, managers monitor the quality of the software products and customer satisfaction . . . Schedules and budgets are based on historical performance and are realistic; the expected results for cost, schedule, functionality, and quality of the product are usually achieved." (Technical Report SEI-93-TR-24)

It will up to the PMO, in the future, to assess the organization's processes, IT and otherwise, to ensure that maturity is being achieved through continuous process improvement, as we Run the Business and also Change the Business. Several assessment tools and techniques are available today to perform ongoing assessments of organizations, including PMI's Organizational Project Management Maturity Model (OPM3®). OPM3® focuses on the effective implementation of Portfolio, Program, and Project Management processes in an organization. This is how we know if OPM is being implemented properly and all portfolios, programs, and projects are properly aligned with the company's business strategies.

In our quest to make changes happen on target, on time, and on budget, it is easy to see how alteration of FET might be a weak link in change if those alterations were being done by an IT organization with immature software processes. Our recommendations for handling different levels of maturity and different degrees of needed alteration are shown in very general form in the following table:

		Software Alterations	
		Simple and Small	Big and Complex
IT Organization	Mature	Use in-house IT resources	Consider using in-house IT resources supplemented by mature outside vendor
IT Organization	Immature	Do with in-house resources only if you use the best IT performers	Use mature outside vendor only

The chart above is probably clear enough to send the strong message that IT maturity is a requirement for altering software that is to be a part of an organizational change intended to be on target, on time, and on budget. One point of explanation might be useful for simple, small changes done in-house in an immature IT organization. For this case, it is very important to get the very best IT resources in the organization on the software alteration project. Odds are they will not use systematic software processes . . . but they probably will do the best job in the IT organization of improvising the software solution.

Testing new and altered FET

We tested altered work processes in an earlier transition step. Now we must test new or altered FET to ensure that it will be ready to play its part in the organizational change. If the key principles are used in altering the physical FET, testing of the final FET and its installation will be done as a part of the project close out. Sounds like an easy-enough answer to our testing requirement, doesn't it?

Beware of the testing done at the close out of the project . . . whether it be for physical or software FET. Those are needed tests, and they likely will be done correctly as part of a disciplined alteration, but they don't go far enough. What is needed here are tests of the FET in the context of the actual work processes that require those particular tools. Our recommendation is to use members of the work process alteration and FET alteration teams to conduct a real-life test of the FET using the altered processes defined earlier. A further step would be to use employees who will actually be using the FET (and not just the "super users") with the altered process when the intended change is finally put into effect.

Tests of the altered FET almost always produce observations from the test participants that point to the need for further alterations of the FET. Change leaders will need to differentiate between those suggested alterations that are learning-curve based or preferences/styles-based rather than process-requirements based. Learning curve based suggestions may be driven more by the test subjects' unfamiliarity with the FET than with actual FET inadequacy. If we discover major needed alterations at this point . . . we haven't been doing something right!

PPI quickly found out that identifying the need for an ERP was a piece of cake compared to its actual implementation. Actual implementation of the system was problematic at first as different functional organizations reacted to the new system. For example, when the marketing and sales folks realized that the new ERP would replace their beloved marketing /sales system, they howled that the new system was inferior to the one they had been using. On the other hand, the production folks saw the new system as far superior to what they had been using and could hardly wait for implementation to be completed. Go figure.

OPM NOTE 3B

In order to show company results the way the CEO wanted them, several changes were needed in the reporting formats that were being used in accounting and finance. The changes were completed quickly and the new reporting formats with RTB and CTB progress were shown side-by-side in the CEO's second month on the job. For the CTB side of the reports, for example, the metrics of numbers of orders shipped on time and received on time (data was already being collected by the company but was only visible within the company's supply chain department).

On a technical note, the RTB/CTB method calls for different kinds of CTB measures. For example, rather than showing "% of on-time shipments" each month, they might have shown the progress of the change Project Team working to design process improvements that, if implemented, would have increased the percentage of on-time shipments. So "percent of project completion" would have been a more appropriate measure.

Requirement 3C: Alter and test FET controls

Mind-Clearing Example—Imagine a Lighting Director who ensures that all the right lights are in place and focused on the stage but who does not alter or test the lighting "control panel" that is still set up for the last production!

So far we have altered work processes and purchased/altered and tested the FET required for use in those altered processes. In this step, the change leader's job is to ensure that the controls on the FET will allow the performance called for by the work process. FET controls are those devices that allow the operators of the FET to make the equipment do what it needs to do, when it needs to do it, in order to perform the work called for by work processes. Sometimes limitations have been set on FET controls that limit the overall performance of the FET.

A simple real-world example of FET control might be the throttle on a truck. Some trucks have a device called a governor installed on the engine. A governor artificially limits the speed of the engine to some speed well within the truck's operating limits. If that truck is moved to the kind of work that requires a higher speed than the one set on the governor, the truck driver will not be able to drive the truck to the goals of the work process.

The job of the change leader is to ensure that control devices on altered equipment are adjusted to meet new process requirements, and that control devices on new equipment provide the operating envelope needed by the work processes. While the FET tests in the previous step will pick up control limitations on the specific FET tested, all duplicate and equipment will need to be physically inspected to ensure it is set within the needed operating parameters.

PPI Example 3C: Alter and test FET Controls

After a lot of hard work, PPI Information Technology professionals aided by outside vendors were able to prepare and configure the ERP system to meet many of the nomenclature needs of the PPI users. After two round of testing, the ERP system went live to find business side users ready to use it.

Tests of the controls for the new rail switch on the new section of track were performed by the engineering vendor who installed the track. Testing was done under the supervision of the Director of Supply Change Management and his staff. Then, as often happens, the Supply Chain guys liked the new high-tech switch panel and its accompanying instrumentation so much that they retained the vendor to install similar instrumentation for the original rail siding.

OPM NOTE 3C

The FET control alterations related to OPM consisted of tests of the upgraded Project Management software. As a result of the tests, the Project Management software vendor was engaged to provide macros to eliminate several of the steps that users needed to take to see the reports they needed.

The Director of Quality and one line manager had reacted when they recognized the number of steps users had to take for reports. Their thought was that any obstacle to the use of the PM software would have been a discouragement to the way the company had committed to manage change.

Requirement 3D: Alter or create operating guidelines for all involved FET

Mind-Clearing Example—Imagine a Lighting Director who ensures that all the right lights are in place for an up-coming play, but who leaves the checklist and operator notes from the last play in place on the lighting panels. Imagine the lighting director missing one performance of the new play and being replaced with a temporary employee who could only see one set of operating instructions on the panel.

Organizations use operating guidelines to guide workers through the proper use of FET. An operating guideline is nothing more than a written set of instructions that describes what workers should and should not do in operation of a particular piece of FET. Operating guidelines are usually provided by the original equipment manufacturers (OEM) of the FET. Operating guidelines are not the same as procedures for work processes.

To avoid any confusion between the two terms, let's look at an example of operating guidelines for simple equipment and the work procedures that call for the use of that equipment

- The copier in our office had the following operating guidelines attached to the top of the machine:

  1. Do not replenish toner before the "Add Toner" lamp flashes
  2. When replenishing toner, add only one cartridge of toner.

- Meanwhile, we had several work procedures that involved the use of that copier:

  1. Take the original of your expense form 3440 to the department's Ricoh copier
  2. Enter your department's copier code first (to get a code, contact Wayne at extension 2880)
  3. Make 3 copies of the expense form 3440 and return the copies to the admin desks in work areas.

For some FET, we have seen extensive operating guidelines, usually provided by the OEM, available at each machine, and we have also seen the other extreme . . . three-line operating guidelines in the form of "crib notes" affixed to the equipment itself.

The important thing about operating guidelines is not necessarily how many there are but how usable they are. We have found that most operating guidelines provided by OEM are not only skimpy and poorly-written, but user unfriendly! The exception to this general finding is FET that has a possible loss of life associated with it. In those cases, operating guidelines are much better written and user friendly.

Most companies develop additional operating guidelines beyond those produced by the OEM. Sometimes these additional operating guidelines are written down, but unfortunately, most times they are not. So around existing FET there is frequently an unwritten body of operating guidelines that is important to the organization's knowledge of how to use the FET.

Given this background of poorly written instructions and unwritten guidelines, leaders of a change initiative must still divine a way to make change happen on target, on time and on budget. Therefore, the critical challenges for dealing with FET operating guidelines are as follows:

- **Challenge One: For new FET, supplement the OEM-provided operating guidelines with your organization's standard additions.** This means that the operating guidelines that come with the newly-purchased FET should not be accepted as all that is needed. As a part of the installation and test of the new FET, make it a priority to write additional operating instructions as needed to come up to the standard that your organization already provides on existing FET.

- **Challenge Two: For existing FET that needs to be altered, change the operating guidelines in writing.** If the impending organizational change calls for the modification of existing FET, the task to get operating guidelines in order will be to document the written and unwritten guidelines already in use for the FET before modification—and then re-write those guidelines for the altered equipment. We have found it effective to sometimes write out the new guidelines on the same document with visible "marks through" of the specific guidelines no longer to be used.

Testing of operating guidelines for new FET and altered guidelines for existing FET is critical to change. The only way we will know that new guidelines will lead to the right results is to test the newly-written guidelines with employees from the populations that will be expected to use them. We recommend what we call a split test to get the most useful information about operating guidelines.

Make sure that the new operating guidelines are identified with an "effective date" or a "revised date." Also consider some special marking, border, or color that catches the workers' eyes and lets them know that new operating guidelines are in place. Once again, new guidelines are of no value unless we get them into the hands of the people who will need to use them in their day-to-day work. (See Requirement 2D in Chapter Five.)

PPI Example 3D: Create operating guidelines

Specific equipment operating guidelines were written and tested for operation of the new rail switch and the accompanying control panel. While the vendor who constructed the new track left the operating manuals for all purchased equipment used in the new track, the company was left with "a pile of stuff," as one manager put it. One Supply Chain professional and one staff member from the Quality Department were tasked by one of the Program Managers to draft the needed operating guidelines in coordination with the Project Improvement team assigned to work on customer shipments. The end result was that the operating guidelines were written, checked, and integrated into the new work procedures being written by the shipment team.

OPM NOTE 3D

PPI needed very few changes in the operating guidelines of the FET that was changed to accommodate OPM. Most of the new guidelines written had to do with the changes in reporting formats (i.e., how to keep formats straight and how to operate some elements of the ERP that had been implemented).

Requirement 3E: Eliminate old FET and operating guidelines

Mind-Clearing Example—Imagine a Lighting Director who instructs her technicians to leave the "lighting level marks" from the last production taped on the lighting panels, mixed in with the level marks for the new play.

Or imagine a Stage Manager who leaves all of the props from the last play in the same prop racks along with the new props for the new play.

The bottom line for this FET requirement is simple to say but more difficult to follow: we must get equipment we no longer want to use out of the organization. The undesired FET must be destroyed or put where people can't get their hands on it . . . or it will be used!

The bottom line for operating guidelines is equally simple but much harder to follow. Essentially we want to have operating guidelines that are no longer relevant, needed, or correct taken out of use in the organization. This simple task is made complex by the fact that many of the operating guidelines that are being used at any one point in time are not written down. It is always tough to get a written policy, procedure, or guideline out of play. It is especially difficult to take unwritten guidelines out of play! But it can be done. The steps we recommend are as follows:

1. Identify the FET operating guidelines that need to be eliminated
2. Create a written draft of any unwanted guidelines that have not been written down (create the draft from what is already written along with information from folks who know the unwritten rules)
3. Get everybody a copy of the "now written" unwanted guidelines
4. Call their attention to the now-written version
5. Tell everybody that those operating guidelines will no longer be used
6. Take the copies away from them, and
7. Destroy the copies letting everybody see you do the destruction!

The commercial airline pilots we discussed in Chapter Five not only systematically deal with changes in work processes and procedures; they also deal with changes in the operating guidelines for the equipment on the aircraft they fly on a daily basis. Not only do pilots systematically remove all old operating guidelines from their flight reference guide, but they systematically examine the cockpits of the aircraft to ensure that there are no lingering operating guidelines present. They have learned that following an old operating guide can really blow up in their faces!

PPI Example 3E: Eliminate old operating guidelines

The CEO was known to be an insistent leader who followed through thoroughly on made decisions. He insisted that the old ways be left behind as PPI moved forward.

While the entire organization followed through on the "in with the new, out with the old" policy, Marketing and Sales discontinued their complaining and changed to a new tactic . . . making a convincing business case for more and different functionality. The CEO bought their proposal and authorized a marketing and sales software package that could "sit on top" of the ERP and provide much of the requested functionality.

A major task was to find all the operating guidelines from the original marketing and sales system. They were found both in offices and online . . . then destroyed leaving only the ERP and new software operating guidelines for staff use. The last major task was to find and remove old guidelines for managing the rail traffic on the company's siding.

OPM NOTE 3E

Fortunately there were only a dozen or so engineers and project managers who had been using the company's old project management application. The Director of Quality and

And in conclusion . . .

Our task in this chapter has been to focus on the third requirement for transitioning an organization: the physical alteration of the organization's FET. Every organizational change is likely to require new or altered FET to enable the altered work processes designed to fulfill the vision. Regardless of the kind of organizational change or the stimulus for organizational change, we work with the assumption that FET alterations will be required . . . unless proven otherwise.

Just as process steps and procedures go together, FET and operating guidelines go together. These guidelines are the written instructions for proper use and operation of FET, be it a ladder, a piece of earth moving equipment or new software. Failing to provide proper operating guidelines for new or altered FET is akin to expecting a new look from a play that is opening with the old set and old costumes from the last play.

Chapter Seven

Altering Performance Management

Mind-Clearing Example—Imagine the Director who talks to the theater company about the new play but fails to put any of the actors under contract for their involvement in that play.

Imagine that every time the actors try to get closure on what their individual roles will be, the Director says, "Just hang on, I'm sure we'll be able to work something out as we go along."

Theater professionals know that no play lasts forever. They also know that transitioning to a new play is the only way they can stay employed. The key mechanism used to transition actors from one play to the next is the "contract" that formalizes the agreement between actor and the theater company to work together, under certain terms, in the next play. In business language, we might say that the Director is "managing the performance of actors" through selecting them for specific roles in a play and putting them (the actors) under contract.

In business, official, signed contracts are not used to manage performance of the vast majority of a workforce. In a business workforce, performance is managed through "agreements to work and agreements to compensate."

- The worker agrees to perform a job that the company has specified, and
- The company agrees to provide the agreed-to compensation to the employee in return for that job performance.

In an organizational change, members of the workforce will be asked to agree to accept a different assignment . . . to perform a different job or an "altered job" in order to continue to receive compensation from the company. It all comes down to this. Failing to alter the performance management system while expecting successful organizational change is akin to expecting the performance of a new play from actors who are still under exclusive contract for performing the old play!

For successful organization change, there must be physical alteration of the performance management system that the organization uses to assign and reinforce the performance of its managers and employees. This performance management system is the organization's mechanism for procuring, directing, and retaining the kind of performance it needs. This performance management system must be altered in order to reinforce the transition to the new way of doing business and to dis-incentivize failure to transition to that new way.

For successful organizational change, employees must be "under agreement" to perform their:

- **New roles** after changeover to the new way of doing business (e.g., agreeing to perform in a new engineering position, to become the operator of new equipment, to head a newly-created department, etc.)

In addition, all employees must be under agreement to perform during the organization's transition to the new way of doing business. During that transition they will perform their:

- **Current roles**, (their "day job" of selling products, serving customers, completing the October financials, etc.)
- **Transition work** (attending training, helping to re-write procedures, testing and calibrating new equipment, etc.)

This performance break-out looks good, doesn't it? But getting these roles all sorted out is easier said than done.

> **Very Important Note to the Reader!! Detour stars here!!**
>
> *As the title of this chapter says, our primary focus will be on managing the transition of employees from one way of doing business to another.*
>
> *HOWEVER, we have learned the hard way that most of us carry a set of assumptions about managing employees that are just plain destructive to organizational change.*
>
> *On the other hand, most of us have our heads straight about contractor performance. Therefore, we will take a detour and first talk about how we manage contractors or vendors in order to convey what we see as the "right mindset" to use with employees as we transition them from one way of doing business to another.*

We can categorically state that one of the most stubborn obstacles to successful organizational change we have seen is the way managers handle "work agreements" in the organization. While altering the organization's physical FET seems to be the best-done part of organizational change, altering the performance management system of the organization seems to be the most difficult by far.

Every organization has a performance management system of some kind whether it is formal and explicit or informal and unwritten. There are two classic performance management systems that organizations use to steer the performance of the people they employ. The first system, (the detour we mentioned in the box above) frequently called "contractor management," is used for steering the performance of those workers whom the company considers as outside contractors or vendors.

The second mechanism, the employee performance management system, is used for steering the performance of those persons whom the organization considers as full or part-time employees. Interestingly enough, theatre companies will frequently use both: contractor management for actors and an employee performance management system for everyone else. As we said earlier, our focus in this chapter is primarily on employee management systems, but please allow us to detour and cover contractor performance first.

Managing contractor performance: the Detour begins!

Most organization members are generally familiar with the way contractors will be managed (after all, most everybody has engaged a "contractor" to mow his lawn, put down new flooring in the kitchen, or complete her tax return.) Any contractor management system, including the one we use informally at home, includes such logical but critical steps as follows:

1. Defining the desired work a contractor is to perform
2. Locating, negotiating, and reaching agreement with a contractor to perform the desired work
3. Explaining the work to be done to the contractor and ensuring understanding
4. Familiarizing the contractor with the way the company works
5. Authorizing the contractor to begin work
6. Monitoring the contractor's performance over the length of the job
7. Ensuring that the contractor has completed the required work and
8. Ensuring the contractor is paid in accordance with the negotiated agreement.

The primary administrative vehicle used in contractor management is the written contract. This instrument, signed by both the contractor and a representative of the organization, contains key sections that are necessary to ensure the agreement is carried out with integrity: the contractor completes the defined work for the organization . . . and the organization provides agreed-to compensation for the work done.

Expect to see the following key sections in a "contractor's contract:"

- Statement of Work—identifies precisely what the contractor is to do for the organization during the specified time period of the contract

- Qualifications—specifies what skills and capabilities the contractor is required to bring to the assignment
- Performance Evaluation—tells the contractor how his performance will be monitored, measured, and evaluated
- Payment—spells out the agreed-to payment terms and conditions for the contract work that is performed satisfactorily
- General Terms—describes how the contractor and organization will do business together during the contract period, including how disputes will be handled.

Contracting for vendor performance is normally handled by the organization's procurement function or Human Resources department. The day-to-day management of the vendor is usually handled by an operating manager who is using the vendor's services in designated work (i.e., the accounting department head specifies the work of a contract accountant). This employing manager directs the vendor's performance as necessary through the terms of the contract.

As the work needs of the organization change, the manager works with the contracting officer and the vendor to modify and re-negotiate the statement of work in the vendor contract. The manager works in this fashion, keeping the vendor and the contract aligned with the work requirements of the organization . . . until there is no longer a need for the services of the contractor. At completion of the agreed-to work, the contract is terminated, and the contractor and the organization go their separate ways to work together again in the future . . . or to never work together again.

End of Detour!

At this point we are back on track to cover the focus of this chapter: Altering Performance Management for Employees. Hopefully we have conveyed two important aspects of organizational change management that will apply to managing the performance of employees:

- **Workers must be under contract or agreement to do the work specified by the company**
- **Workers must be compensated for satisfactorily performing their agreed-to work.**

Managing employee performance

In practical terms, employee performance can be managed very much like contractor performance. An employee must be "under agreement" to do the work of the organization in order to receive the rewards for work. When we use the term "contract" with employees, we are usually not talking about a written contract like that used with vendors. In practice, very few employees have formal written contracts but they must be "under agreement" with the organization.

The point is that all employees work under an agreement with the company (the equivalent of a contract): employees agree that they are to do certain things for the organization in order to be paid. The company agrees to pay x amount for y work, while the employee agrees to do y work for x amount.

The steps we take to get employees under agreement and to work for the company are similar to the steps we take with contractors. We must systematically and responsibly take the following interrelated steps when we manage employee performance:

1. Think through what work we want an employee to do.
2. Find (or have Human Resources find) an employee who has the skills, capabilities, and initiative necessary to do that work.
3. Assign and communicate the specific work to the employee, and secure her understanding and willingness to do the work.
4. Formalize the agreement to work together with proper hiring paperwork, a handshake, and "welcome aboard" speech.
5. Provide any final training needed by the employee to be able to do the work.
6. Have the employee begin work . . . including taking personal initiative to perform to the needed level.

7. Ensure the employee gets feedback on how her work is progressing.
8. Evaluate employee performance and ensure the employee is properly/fairly paid for his/her services under the hiring agreement.

Our key message is a simple one: for long-term success in employee performance management, employees must always be under agreement to do the work of the company. And as the requirements of the work change, it is up to the employing manager to keep an up-to-date agreement with employees in effect at all times.

> For example, let's say that an employee has been under agreement to do tasks "A through F" in a company department. Let's say that the work needed in that department changes, for whatever reason. It is up to the employing manager to get the employee under agreement to do the new work—say, tasks "B through H." The employing manager follows the steps shown above—from understanding the new work, through communicating the new work to the employee; gaining his understanding and agreement to start two new tasks, stop doing one old task and to continue doing the remainder of the old tasks; providing training as needed for the new tasks; starting the new employee to work on the new tasks; providing feedback to the employee on performance; and ensuring that the employee's performance is fully evaluated at the end of the year and that the employee is properly paid for doing the new job and not the old one.

As in the case of vendor management, the employing manager works with representatives of the Human Resources department for assistance in completing the basic steps in managing employee performance. While the details may vary from company to company, it is critical for the employing managers and the Human Resource managers to come to their own clear agreement on how they will work together to ensure effective and efficient employee performance management.

Identify and dispel deadly assumptions about altering performance management

The step of transitioning the performance management system to enable an organization to move to a new way of doing business is among the most challenging tasks that managers face in change. Why most challenging? It seems simple enough. Because somehow we feel that making changes in an employees work will "hurt the employee and stress us out." This assumption may be one that managers want to make since they see it as making their jobs easier and less stressful at the interpersonal level.

From a mechanical point of view, altering performance management is relatively simple, but from an interpersonal point of view, it is one of the most dreaded tasks that many managers must take on. Most managers do not look forward to talking to their direct reports about new standards of performance, about changes in the way performance will be evaluated, or about changing compensation arrangements. (At the same time, many of those managers would not bat an eye about changing the work agreement with a contractor!)

Step	Change-Blocking Assumptions	Disabling Behavior	Proven Consequences
Requirement Four: Transitioning the Performance Management System	Changing their work will: • Be hurtful for employees and • Unpleasant for me. • "After all, this change is about their work, not what we pay."	• Talking about change without connecting change to employee evaluation and compensation • Failure to alter either job descriptions or compensation payoffs • Failure to be proactive about performance short-falls or failures	• Unwillingness to change • Lowered Morale • Poor performance

Consequently, this assumption allows managers to dodge the real truth that must be conveyed to employees in an organizational change: "We are making a change, your job will be different, your evaluation will be done against your new job, not the old one, and your compensation will be directly linked to your level of performance in the new way of doing business."

Hearing the suggestion to "Leave the employees alone; we don't need to talk to them about pay; that's a hot subject and they will all get on board as we go along" gives away the presence of deadly assumptions and calls for the change leader to dispel them in any way possible, starting with the proven consequences in the table above.

Take these Action Steps to Complete Requirement Four: Altering Performance Management

Failure to alter performance management will literally stop an organizational change in its tracks. Take the following five steps to transition performance management:

Action steps to transition performance management

- 4A: Identify and alter individual roles
- 4B: Complete one-on-one contracting with all affected employees
- 4C: Train all employees in the new roles they will play
- 4D: Identify and alter the system for evaluating performance
- 4E: Alter and communicate communication payoffs

Requirement 4A: Identify and alter individual roles and goals needed for change

Mind-Clearing Example—Imagine a Director who can't decide how many dancers will be in the chorus line for his new musical. Imagine the Director responding to one of the dancers: "I don't know if you will be in the line or not. Just work your way in somewhere and we'll see what develops!"

Or imagine a Director who has decided she wants a certain actor in the new production but who is unwilling to decide which of three roles might be the best use of the actor's talent!

We use an organization's performance management system to both guide employee performance and then to ensure the employee is paid for his performance. This step in engineering the performance management system is all about identifying the specific roles and goals that workers will need to develop and play after an organizational change. Just as each actor in a play must have a role, so must each and every employee. We define "role" as an organization member's job, his assigned set of tasks and responsibilities. (From our earlier discussion of performance management, an employee's role is his agreed-to statement of work that he is paid to accomplish.)

In addition to job descriptions, workers need specific targets or goals for designated time periods. We want to set specific goals and objectives for individual and team performance to meet the needs of the process objectives already set in Requirement Two: Altering Work Processes. We want to have specific measures that can be monitored by both workers and managers to understand and manage the level of worker performance in his new role after the change.

Change requires new or altered roles and goals

The job for the change leader is first and foremost to identify what roles will be needed to fulfill the vision of the new way of doing business. He then must identify the goals that need to be associated with each role to meet the level of performance expected in the new way of doing business. Then the change leader must identify which new roles will be needed (with accompanying goals), which existing roles will need to change (the direction of those changes), and what roles will not change . . . and then communicate that information personally to everybody in the organization. Now this sounds simple . . . and it is. But it can become a big job since some organizations have many managers and employees to get into new roles or to "steady" in their old roles (i.e., the current roles of some employees will not be altered as a part of an organization change, and they should be told that).

Regardless of the kind of organizational change or the stimulus for organizational change, new roles and goals or alterations of some existing roles and goals will be required.

- If an organization decides to **change its business strategy** to become the high safety service provider, for example, many, if not all, of the organization's work processes will need to change to take out waste and risk-prone non-standard steps or to alter the sequence of steps, and so on. In addition, the company's marketing processes would need to be altered to add promotional steps and materials that stress changed features and outcome measures of the organization's service delivery. This kind of strategy change will require that people do work differently (i.e., have their roles and goals altered) in accordance with the new work processes.

- If an organization decides to **change one of the technologies** that it uses in its business, role and goal alterations are almost certain to be involved. Work steps to set-up the new FET and to use the output of the new system will need to be assigned to somebody (i.e., become a part of their roles in the company). A new software tool, for instance, will likely require either new data elements to enter the software and/or new steps to use the output of the software requiring alteration of the roles and goals of the assigned workers.

- If an organization decides to make **a change in its culture**, several process changes will result as organization members begin to approach the job differently. If, for example, the desired cultural change is to become more attentive to customers, changes will probably need to be made in the steps used in the design of customer service into the work processes, behavior styles and feedback systems . . . impacting the roles and goals of the organization members assigned to those Departments.

We believe that the primary tool for changing an organization's culture is the performance management system. Culture change begins with the revision of employee roles to include the desired behaviors wanted in the new culture followed by compensation rules that pay off for workers using the desired behaviors.

- If an organization decides to make **a change in its organizational structure**, alterations will likely be required both in management/ decision-making processes as well as in the work processes performed by members of the units that are involved. These process alterations will result in role alterations for managers and workers alike. (Note: We have seen companies make many changes to their organization structures that were entirely superficial in nature, leading to no substantial changes to the four mechanical attributes emphasized in this book. To us, an organization change should be focused on bringing better resourcing . . . of people and skills . . . to bear on substantial changes to work processes. In short, we tell our clients to forget about changing the organizational structure if they do not intend to make work processes more effective or efficient.)

This first step in transitioning the organization's performance management system is to identify a role and goal for everybody in the new way of doing business. Everyone must have an identified role and goal for performance for the organization to make its change. However, as we said earlier, for many organizational changes, the roles and goals of some employees will remain unchanged.

Use a team to identify new and altered organizational roles and goals

We want to finish this step with four end products:

1. a list of the new roles that will be needed,
2. a list of current roles that will need to be altered, along with
3. the direction/nature of the required alterations, and
4. a list of the organizational roles that will not need to be altered to enact the vision.

We generate these lists from analysis of four resources:

- List of work processes to be altered
- List of FET to be altered
- The organization chart and accompanying tables, and
- The organization's master listing of personnel.

The first step in identifying needed role and goal alterations (and/or new roles) is to systematically go through the organization's altered work processes and FET to visualize any modifications that will be needed in roles and goals for organization members. In previous steps . . . alteration of work processes (Chapter Five) and alteration of FET (Chapter Six) . . . we generated lists entitled: "process alterations needed to reach the vision" and "FET alterations needed to reach the vision." These lists are the obvious starting places for identifying role and goal alterations or new roles.

Support workers as they develop needed roles and goals

Mind-Clearing Example—Imagine an actor who has just signed a contract for a role in a new play. Imagine that actor reading the script to better understand his role . . . and then waiting for the director to come around and tell him exactly how to play each detail of the part.

When asked about his approach, the actor says, "Hey, I just go on stage and do what I have been told to do." Want to bet on that actor's chances of survival in the professional theater world?

Organizations should expect that workers will take the needed initiative to develop their new or altered roles . . . when cued by their bosses to do so. A boss must make it a given that her workers will exercise the personal responsibility needed to develop (fill out the details) of the new roles needed in the new way of doing business. Fortunately most employees will take that initiative and work out their own details.

Experience has taught us that change leaders need to orchestrate the role development process to ensure that all workers get their needed role and goal alterations identified and made. Failure to use a firm hand to ensure that such work gets done will inevitably produce great variance in scheduled completion of the alterations (many workers will be late if left to their own devices) as well as great variation in the thoroughness and level of detail of role descriptions and documentation.

An approach that has worked for us for years is as simple as this: we encourage old pro employees to develop their own needed roles and goals alterations with little assistance from the boss. On the other hand, we recommend that the boss take the lead in developing the roles and goals of rookie employees who are new to the work of the company. Regardless of who works through the alterations, those alterations still need to be done on schedule for the change to happen as expected.

In the end, it is each individual worker who will have to work through the details of his role and goals in order to meet the expectations of the organization after the change. But change leaders do need to take firm control of the process of identifying and ensuring role and goal alterations to have any real chance to have the organizational change . . . on target, on time, and on budget.

The PMO will be instrumental in helping to define new roles, responsibilities, and related training. The PMO will also need to coordinate the training program for project managers and project personnel. The implementation of OPM will require new roles, such as portfolio managers, program managers, risk and scheduling professionals. These new roles don't yet exist in many organizations and carrying out change will become extremely difficult in their absence.

> **PPI Example 4A.1: Identify and alter individual roles and goals:**
> **Developing roles**
>
> As the direction of recommendations for process changes began to crystallize inside both Programs and Projects, the PPI Executive Team began to look ahead to identify where changes in roles would be needed. They found several obvious jobs/roles throughout the company that were directly related to

customer service that needed to be changed to align with the vision of Perfect Service. Other roles had to be changed as well, for example, changes in duties and responsibilities in the Supply Chain part of the organization.

PPI had an active Human Resources function that handled employee matters in a disciplined way. In fact, the Director of Human Resources had been an active member of the Program and Project system to stay in the loop and to ensure that HR policies were honored. When the need for modification of job descriptions was obvious, the HR Director and his staff were directly involved in re-shaping job descriptions and goals. HR did not take the stance of "here is why we can't do that to that description" but instead adopted the stance of "here is how we can get that done." The CEO's idea was to keep HR formally in the loop from the moment the organizational change was initiated.

OPM NOTE 4A

A number of role and job description changes were required for use of the RTB/CTB method. All management job descriptions were modified to include phrases like the following:

- To lead your assigned department to the business results identified by your management and the year's operational plan and budget.
- To plan for and lead your department to make changes that are aligned with overall corporate change initiatives, being responsible for communicating change directions, putting in place new processes, technology, and job roles
- To lead your Department personnel in continuous improvement, striving for excellence in the functions your Department provides for the organization

> The CTB role of the Director of Quality was fleshed out by the incumbent working directly with the CEO. As we stated earlier, the role that was developed over time was focused on what we would today call the Manager of the PMO.
>
> The role of the Quality Director was defined with two key thrusts: (1) implementing and supporting the RTB /CTB way of doing business and (2) implementing and supporting a Baldrige-backed Quality Improvement methodology. When the two thrusts were combined, the portfolio of improvement projects for a given year was identified and managed using the RTB/CTB method while each project used the Baldrige-backed methods for work process improvement.
>
> PPI made a conscious decision to minimize staff in the office of the Quality Director. Their ideas was "not to do" all of the functions needed to support RTB/CTB, but "to get the functions done" through or with other PPI managers and professionals.

Document the new and altered roles and goals

Companies vary in the ways they handle the contents of roles of organization members. Some companies have written roles and goals for their positions and some do not. While there is great variation among companies, the most popular device for recording the contents of roles is the job description with an accompanying annual goals list. Our bottom line is simple, we don't really care what kind of device the company uses to document roles. We just recommend that there be such a device, and that it be used systematically. The written job description with accompanying goals for the new and altered roles is the equivalent of the new statement of work that will be expected from vendors or employees after the change over to the new way of doing business.

Determine the compensation level for new and altered roles

The last critical part of the role alteration step is to determine the compensation level that matches the new and altered roles needed for the new way of doing business. It will do no good to offer an employee an altered role if the offered compensation is not enough to get the employee to accept it. This critical step to determine compensation must be initiated by the change leader assisted by a representative from Human Resources. That HR representative must ensure that the altered roles and the determined compensation for those roles fit with the company's normal Human Resources Compensation policy and procedures (which normally include benchmarking pay in the local job market):

- **No compensation change for typical role alteration:** If the altered role still fits within the same job classification (and labor market), the organization should not need to change compensation for the role. In fact, one of our key goals in identifying needed role alterations is to keep jobs within the same families and classification ranges.

- **No pay for routine change:** An organization cannot give extra compensation, a raise or a bonus, for every change an organization might make in the way it does business. If a company were forced to pay everyone an extra amount for every change, that company would soon find itself with a cost structure that would be out of line with the market place. A key idea is that once organizations and individuals have mastered change, they will both be willing and able to make normal changes without a great deal of support, attention, and without feeling that extra compensation is due.

- **Pay for role alterations that significantly change the employment situation:** Occasionally, when organizations alter jobs so that more or higher skills are involved in the new work, it may be necessary to adjust the employee's compensation package. Some companies, for example, have procedures for grading jobs on difficulty, the level of accountability for results, the number of people supervised, etc. If role alterations move an employee to a new salary classification level, the company will need to be pro-actively prepared to pay for it.

PPI Example 4A.2: Identify and alter individual roles and goals

CEO: "We set two kinds of hard targets that year and every year thereafter: Run-the-Business targets including safety record, cash flow, return on capital employed, and customer satisfaction. We set stiff Change-the-Business targets for (1) improving customer perception of reliability and (2) achieving "Perfect Service" (0% late deliveries, 0% complaints, 0% incorrect invoices).

The CEO through the Executive Team ensured that every manager in the organization had individual goals that aligned with goals at the company level including the Perfect Service initiative.

CEO: Bottom-Line business metrics were chosen. We decided to use metrics that meant something to the business world (e.g. customer satisfaction ratings, profitability margin). We wanted formally-defined, bullet-proof measures, not ones "we could fudge." We used objective, industry third-party services and external auditors/examiners for our metric information.

OPM NOTE 4A.2

The CEO, working with the Director of Human Resources, directed that RTB/CTB role adjustments be formally made for all PPI managers. In the next few weeks, the RTB/CTB requirement was communicated by the CEO and his executive team to all PPI managers.

A second step was to modify Management job descriptions and performance appraisal forms and criteria to include the responsibilities for RTB/CTB. The responsibilities for RTB and CTB were given equal weight and emphasis. There it was, in black and white, the news that all managers were then accountable to do both.

Requirement 4B: Complete one-on-one contracting with every worker

Mind-Clearing Example—Imagine a Director who is ready to begin rehearsals for a new play but who has not put any of the actors under contract for the play. Imagine the Director getting feedback that the actors wanted their contracts signed . . . but who stated, "Tell them not to worry . . . I've always been a man of my word!"

When an organization changes, some people will have different jobs. Jobs may be anything from almost the same as before the change to radically different. When we want workers to do that different job, we must put them under agreement to do so. And when we need other workers to keep doing their old jobs into the new organization, we need to confirm their agreement to do so. To make things more difficult, we must get folks into new agreements and confirming old agreement on a one-on-one basis.

Workers in an existing organization are usually under agreement to do current work. Until that agreement is changed with them, workers will consciously or unconsciously tend to keep doing what they have been doing. Not only do we need to get workers under agreement for the new job, but we must get them to agree to continue the old job until the moment of change-over to the new one. This step in transitioning the performance management system is all about getting a new agreement in place with the workers involved in an organizational change so that they will be willing to perform to expectations. And unlike many other steps in organizational change, the change leader cannot do this step. Only an immediate supervisor can get an employee under a new agreement.

Implementation of the new way of doing business cannot occur until each employee is prepared and under agreement for the performance needed. Terms of the agreement call on each employee to use the altered processes and FET to meet the goals and objectives associated with their position. Getting workers under agreement takes careful preparation, systematic execution of one or more one-on-one contracting sessions, and after-session follow-up to ensure the agreement is sound and can be managed.

Get clear on the agreement that is needed between the organization and the employee

Before meeting with workers on a one-on-one basis, it is critical for the boss to get clear on what he will be trying to accomplish. When this step is completed, we want each worker under agreement to:

- Play a new or modified role in the organization after the change goes into effect (i.e., to act the altered role and meet specific goals in the new way of doing business

- Continue to perform at the needed level in the current job until time to formally change to the new way of doing business

- Do those Change Work transition tasks as required to make all the needed mechanical changes to get to the new role (i.e., help in defining the new role and goals, participating in training and work process walk-throughs, etc.)

- Accept the compensation package and job title that the company will be offering (either changed or unchanged from the present organization)

Get ready for the contracting session

A boss cannot get a worker under a new agreement unless he is under such a new agreement himself! Imagine a Director trying to get actors under contract for a new play when the Director is not sure she has a job! Getting bosses on board first means that contracting will need to be done in an organizational cascade . . . from the top of the units affected by the change to the bottom.

The boss must also be ready to explain the vision, the work process and FET alterations that will be needed for that change . . . and consequently, the role and goal alterations required. Readiness also includes enthusiasm and high expectations for the organizational change. Regardless of the enthusiasm, optimism, and hopes of the CEO or the change leader in the organization, it is the expectations of the employee's immediate boss that count with the employee in the contracting session. Bosses who cannot muster enthusiasm for such sessions with their employees are clearly not under agreement themselves. It is up to each boss to get ready, be ready . . . or go back to her boss and re-contract!

In addition to organizational direction, the boss should be prepared to offer and discuss a fair compensation package that

- The worker is likely to accept and
- The company is able to afford.

The boss should have checked with both the change leader and the organization's Human Resources Department to get clear on the compensation package to be offered and whether or not there is negotiating room on any parts of the package.

The materials the boss will need to have in hand for the one-on-one session with each employee includes the following:

- The relevant role or job description and job title as it will apply under the new way of doing business (frequently the title will be unchanged),
- A statement of individual goals associated with the new way of doing business,
- The organization chart as it will look under the new way of doing business,
- Any team assignments relevant to the new job,
- The offered compensation package, and
- The effective date for the organization change and any changes in compensation

The last and one of the most critical parts of the preparation will be to schedule the worker for the one-on-one session. Schedule a meeting place that will be private during your conversation with the worker, a conversation that could last from 30 minutes to an hour. Be sure to tell the worker that the purpose of the session is to formally invite the worker to be a part of the upcoming organizational change. The worker should have heard about the change multiple times . . . if we have executed our communication plans as outlined in Requirement One: Communicating Vision of the New Way of Doing Business.

Conduct the contracting session to get agreements in place

The contracting meeting is a business meeting, and it needs to have a planned business agenda. The contracting meeting may go as smooth as silk with the employee readily agreeing and getting on board (such is usually the case in organizations that have mastered change). Frequently, however, the process does not go straight through in a 30 minute meeting. The boss may encounter one of the following situations, particularly if the organizational change will be perceived as a major one by the employee.

- **The employee needs time to consider:** If that is the case, agree to meet again with the employee after two or three days. Some employees need the time to consider, or they want to check with a spouse. They may even want to get the reaction of other employees who are going through the contracting session.

- **The employee wants to negotiate:** We are offering, in essence, a different job to the employee. Negotiation should not be a surprise and might be looked on as a normal part of a business transaction. The employee needs to be able to consider the new job along with the offered compensation. The boss must be able to handle the negotiation based on his preparation for the meeting.

- **The employee is unwilling to take the offer:** Some employees may not be willing to take on a new or different role for their own reasons (e.g., the new position calls for a move or the employee's retirement is very near). If so, the boss might want to be respectful of that decision and do what he can to begin to transition the employee out of the current position and into a new place in the organization before the effective time of organizational change.

    Having an employee say, "No, thank you," in a contracting session is not necessarily bad news. If this employee would not have been cooperative in the organizational change, it is better by far that we find out about that in the contracting session and not in the first few weeks of the change when the employee's lack of cooperation could hurt the organization's performance.

- **The Employee is not sure:** Some employees might not be sure whether or not they want to move to an altered position. Some employees may not be able to get rid of their uncertainty until after they are in the altered role. All this is understandable and acceptable, to a point.

    The supervisor should not entertain the idea of letting the employee try the new role without getting the employee to agree to a "100% effort" to do the new role as it needs to be done for the trial period. This agreement to work at 100% is necessary to (1) ensure that the organization can count on the needed performance from that role and so that (2) the employee will really understand and appreciate what the altered role requires . . . and can, therefore, make a better decision about taking the position long-term.

Over the years we have had several managers balk at the contracting idea because, as they said, "You are serving up this organizational change as a take-it or leave-it situation!" Our standard response has become: "Yes, in a way, it is a take-it or leave-it situation. The organization's leadership has decided to make the change. The needed work process alterations and FET alterations are no longer optional. The only thing that is optional is whether or not the current employee chooses to work in the new way of doing business."

Imagine a contracting session between a Director and an actor. When the actor is offered a role in the new play, he says, "No thank you, I like the old play better, and I'll just stick with my part in that play!" A fly on the wall might say, "What play? Hello, the old play has left the building."

Seal the contracting session with a handshake

We shake hands when we buy something. We shake hands when we sell something. We shake hands after a job is offered and accepted. And we shake hands after we have agreement with the employee to move to a new way of doing business. "Let's shake on our new business deal!"

Most companies do not do a good job of changing the agreement with the employee on a one-on-one basis. Companies try to change employee agreements "in batch" with several employees in the same room listening to a big boss explain what the company needs "from each and every one of you!" That's an important speech to make, and we wouldn't do away with it, but I would make sure that the speech is followed by a one-on-one meeting between every affected employee and his boss. In that one-on-one meeting it is up to the boss, representing the employer, to ensure that the employee understands the need from him to do the job differently. It's up to the boss to look into the employee's eyes and confirm agreement to do it the new way . . . and then to consummate the deal with our culture's symbol of agreement—the handshake!

The handshake is the very last act we use to get managers and employees to change to the new direction in the company. The handshake finalizes the re-negotiation of an employee's role in the new future of the organization. The handshake represents the employee's intention to perform to the new role, as he or she understands it . . . for the accepted compensation package. The handshake represents the company's (and management's) intention to expect and support performance of the new role. Last but not least, the handshake cancels the old role agreement between company and employee when the change-over to the new way of doing business occurs.

The handshake, completed under an eyeball-to-eyeball gaze, signals two people's intention to go forward together toward a new way of working. And if either party cannot execute the handshake, everybody knows where they are . . . and they then can solve the problem of lack of agreement—either through more explanation, negotiation, or by transfer or by terminating the relationship.

Record the new agreement

Take that last step and document the organization's records to show that the employee accepted the altered role at the offered or negotiated compensation level. The record should also note whether the acceptance by the employee is for some trial period or the long term. We also recommend that for major organizational changes, the boss pen a letter to the employee thanking him for accepting the altered role in the new organization. Many managers have wished they had such a letter after an employee disavowed any knowledge of the impending change and/or the contracting session with the boss.

OPM NOTE 4B

PPI's CEO did contract with each Executive team member. Given that two changes were going on at once, the CEO ensured that his eye-to-eye gaze and handshake covered both changes.

Requirement 4C: Train all employees in their new roles

Mind-Clearing Example—Imagine a Director who doesn't think the theater company can spare the time for rehearsals.

Or imagine the Director who says, "All the members of my company are experienced stage professionals . . . they certainly don't need to go through the humiliation of rehearsing a play in front of their peers and an empty theater!"

When workers start doing work that is relatively new to them, they need to know what they are doing. How is that for a revolutionary idea? If workers are asked to change to work that they do not know how to do, they will not be able to perform well, and they will probably have feelings of fear, uncertainty, and doubt. This step in altering the performance management system is all about getting the necessary training to workers involved in an organizational change so that they will be able to perform to expectations—theirs and the company's.

Many managers seem to think that training employees for organizational change is no big deal. Actually, we have found a huge amount of confusion around the training that accompanies organizational change. What we want for organization members is the kind of training that theater company members get in their rehearsal for a new play. Employees need training in their roles. Organization members in many of today's organizations have gotten every other kind of training you can think of, without getting any training or rehearsal at all on the roles they are to perform!

We have seen the following training courses offered (or made mandatory) for organization members with good intentions of preparing them for an upcoming organizational change:

- The psychological theory of personal change
- Personality types and how they respond to change
- Stress management
- Learning theory
- Creative thinking and innovation
- The Theory of the learning organization . . . and we could go on!

All the above course titles may be legitimate areas of study . . . they just don't fit well with an organization that is trying to move from the way it operates now to a new way that has been designed for the future. To make our point, consider the following:

> *Mind Clearing Example—Imagine a theatrical director announcing the following to her actors readying for the next play: "I have exciting news! Rather than doing those dreary rehearsals we usually do for a new play, I have booked a professor from Columbia to come in-house to teach us the following courses in lieu of rehearsals:*
>
> - *TA 101: History and theory of the theater*
> - *TA 102: Modern musical comedy in the American Theater*
> - *TA 103: The Economics of the Modern Entertainment Business*
> - *TA 104: Psychological profiles of Actors with Stage Fright"*
>
> *How would you like to hear what the actors have to say about that bright idea? Imagine that their continued requests for rehearsals of the script are answered with even more courses like the ones above (from CCNY this time) instead of intensive focus on the task at hand . . . learning the ins and outs of the play they will be performing in a matter of weeks!*

Yes, training is important for organizational change, but it must be training that directly contributes and counts toward mastery of the new organizational play that is to be performed!

Get clear on the Objectives of Training

The objectives for training in the context of organizational change are clear: we want the workers in the organization to be able to competently perform the work that is required for the new way of doing business that is described in the vision. We want the workers to be able to do their newly-assigned roles at the needed performance levels, whether their roles are new to them or alterations of the roles they currently perform. We want to ensure that individuals will have the knowledge, skills, and attitudes needed to perform to altered statements of work

We want the kind of hands-on training that a theater company gets as it goes through its rehearsals for the new production. Just as we want a cast to run through rehearsal after rehearsal leading up to a final "dress rehearsal," we want workers to be trained to needed performance levels in the roles they will play in the new way of doing business.

Get clear on the Contents of Special Training for OPM

Organizational Project Management calls for specific knowledge, skills and competencies. A position in an OPM organization is a skilled, professional position requiring strong competences in at least three areas as shown in the figure below:

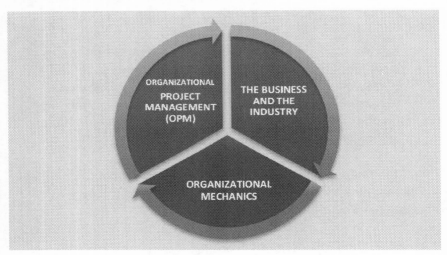

Figure 7.1: Required Competencies for OPM Professionals

- **Organizational Project Management**

Obviously the incumbent in any position in an OPM organization must know OPM . . . beyond the surface-level knowledge we have described in this book. All five aspects of OPM are highly technical areas requiring deep knowledge and experience. The need for advanced skills in OPM positions is certainly clear, given that the purpose of an OPM organization is the translation and planning of actions that will put the company's strategy in place. There is a lot at stake when an organization attempts to implement its selected strategy. A position in an OPM organization is not the place for rookies or neophytes.

- ## The Business and the Industry

OPM professionals must know and appreciate the fine points of the business their company is in. One or more of the OPM professionals needs to be at an expert level in the business . . . "having the business in his bones." Why? Companies in mature industries are technical beasts. Either organizational members know what they are doing and why they are doing it . . . or they are likely to fail. Those OPM professionals must know the business themselves, especially when it comes to Visioning and Portfolio Management or they are likely to misunderstand or miss the nuances of the executive messages they are supposed to be translating and facilitating.

- ## Applied Organizational Mechanics[22]

Organizational Project Management is obviously about organizations and how they need to be changed from time to time to align with company vision and strategy. An OPM Project Manager, therefore, is put in place to assist the organizational change process.

To perform OPM, therefore, requires the application of expertise in complex organizations. The field of Organizational Theory/Mechanics is the branch of *science* concerned with the behavior of *organizations* when subjected to *forces* or *changes*, and the subsequent effects of the organizations on their environment. That means knowledge and skill in strategic planning and implementation, forms of division of labor, work process design, organizational structures, decision making mechanics, performance management, etc.

> **OPM is about the use of Organizational Science to facilitate organizational change.**
> **Don't attempt Organizational Change without it!**

---

[22] Organizations in Action: Social Science Bases of Administrative Theory (Classics in Organization and Management Series) James D. Thompson. 2003

Arrange the needed training

We want to arrange for the training needed to raise knowledge, skills, and attitudes to the levels necessary for satisfactory performance in the new way of doing business. When many managers think about training, they envision classroom training in which workers hear about the new tasks they will need to be able to do in the new way of doing business. While such classroom training is useful for moving the workforce to a level of awareness and preparation for the change, the kind of training that most fills the bill for preparation for organizational change is hands-on, practical training. In practical training, the workers get the opportunity:

- to do actual work
- using the new work processes
- with any new enabling FET
- on a repetitive basis
- until they develop the needed level of proficiency.

The kind of arrangements that organizations need to make to execute training probably needs to vary with the intensity and importance of the organizational change. Obviously when proficiency in work processes or FET is required for safety reasons or critical business consequence reasons, training needs to be intensively applied.

- **High proficiency required:** For critical organizational changes requiring high proficiency of workers as soon as the organizational change goes into effect, training must be systematic, intense, and repetitively delivered. We watched up close and personal both NASA and the US Air Force training its crews to perform a new mission . . . and that training was intense, starting months before the new mission commence date and went on daily until all crews had the needed level of proficiency. In such situations, individual crew members received literally hundreds of hours of training before that had the necessary level of proficiency.

- **Minimum proficiency required:** For organizational changes that only require a minimum level of worker proficiency at the time of the change, training can be applied must less intensively. It is still critical, however, that training move the workforce up to that minimum level before we throw the switch at Change Over. We have seen many organizational changes that involved work process changes with altered computer screens. In many of these changes, the change leaders took the step of arranging some computer-use training before the changeover but then they left the workers to sort out the best use of the software after the change.

- **Learning curve required:** For organizational changes that require a long trip on the learning curve, training must be carefully arranged to get the workforce to the needed level of proficiency within both the schedule and economic constraints of the change. (The learning curve idea has been around since the 1930's and deals with the rate of learning that takes place as workers double the amount of repetition of the job. Industrial engineers can calculate the likely learning rate for the specific operations involved in an organizational change and the training repetitions needed before change-over.)

Conduct the needed training

We want to arrange for the training needed to raise knowledge, skills, and attitudes to the levels necessary for satisfactory performance after the change. When many managers think about training, they envision classroom training in which workers hear about the new things they will need to be able to do in the new way of doing business. While such classroom training is useful for moving the workforce to a level of awareness and preparation for the change, the kind of training that most fills the bill for preparation for organizational change is hands-on, practical training. In practical training, the workers get the opportunity to do actual work using the new processes with the enabling FET on a repetitive basis until they develop the needed level of proficiency.

- The seriousness of your training program sends a signal to workers about the importance of the change to the organization, and therefore to them.

- Use the best trainers, not the folks who are easiest to make available.

- Consider using first line supervisors for trainers because they will be on point for day-to-day, over-the-shoulder coaching and re-training after change-over.

- Don't train so far in advance that the workers "forget before they use."

- Keep to the schedule . . . don't compromise or give up allocated time.

- Continually evaluate how the training is going, and

- Alter training content and schedule as needed to meet the training objectives.

Test workers to ensure readiness to change

OK, so you can't imagine a Director who yells, "Show Time!" before having a full dress rehearsal in which she grades each actor's readiness for opening night. Hopefully, you also can't imagine your airline pilot announcing to his expectant passengers: "I'm really excited about this trip in our new Boeing 787! This will be the very first time I've flown this baby!"

For successful organizational change, we want to test each individual to ensure his capability to perform at the needed level. We have seen organizations where the very use of the word "test" sends off shock waves among the employees . . . and in some cases among employee advocates. We use the word "test" to mean the same thing that the Director does when he views a rehearsal and identifies those actors that need further role development and/or practice. The rehearsal provides information to the Director about what additional coaching and/or repetition she needs to bring to the theater company in transition.

We have also found that it is a good idea to record the training that people have completed and when they pass the proficiency test for the upcoming work. We want to make a permanent record of training and tested performance level. We have had these training records come in handy when we were working with change leaders to understand exactly where they were in a change project they were running or inheriting.

PPI Example 4C: Train All Employees in Their New Roles

Two subjects were covered in organization-wide training on (1) principles and techniques of quality improvement and (2) practical aspects of exceptional customer service. Training was not delivered just once and written off, but was both repeated and expanded on a regular basis.

It is worthy of note that each training session was kicked off by the CEO (. . . or in a rare case, by another member of the Executive Team) who talked about

- the current performance of the company,
- the vision for the future,
- the critical success factors, and
- the importance of training.

He usually concluded with a positive expression of his confidence in the company's future. (NOTE: The CEO is not a fictional character in this book but a real person!)

OPM NOTE 4C

The Director of Quality personally setup the management training need to move the organization forward. Training sessions were held on the subject of Run-the-Business/Change-the-Business, with the training taught by the originator of the RTB/CTB method. (The trainer commented later about how much more responsive an audience seems to be when one of the participants is an energized CEO who asks good questions.

Requirement 4D: Identify and alter the system for monitoring performance

> *Mind-Clearing Examples—Imagine a Director who watches a dozen rehearsals of the new play without giving any feedback to the cast.*
>
> *Or imagine a Director who schedules a rehearsal but who doesn't leave his office to attend it. Imagine the Director saying after the rehearsal, "I want you to get your feedback from your fellow performers."*
>
> *Or imagine a Director who says, "Let's just wait for the audience to give us feedback on how we are doing! They're the best judges anyway!"*

When workers start doing work that is relatively new to them, they need to know how well they are doing. If they do not know how they are doing, their performance may suffer because of uncertainty and/or doubt. Or they may conclude that since they are getting no feedback to the contrary, what they are doing must be right on target! This step in altering the performance management system is all about getting information to workers so that they can feel more comfortable about their work and continue to improve performance.

When workers are in existing jobs for any period of time, they know where they are performance-wise because of the measures provided on the job or from routine feedback from customers or fellow employees. When workers are moved to new or different roles, these old ways of getting feedback are disrupted. Therefore, one of the tasks of the change leader is to ensure that there are means put in place for workers in new jobs to understand how well they are doing and what parts of the job they need to do better.

The most important mechanisms for getting feedback to employees who are new to work are as follows: supervisor input, measurable goals, just-in-time assessment and training, and customer/peer feedback.

- **Supervisor input:** The primary feedback mechanism for new or altered worker performance is the opinion and judgment of the worker's supervisor. Just as the stage performer looks to the Director for signals that she is performing the role as needed in the play, workers look to their bosses to ensure that they are on the right track. If an organization is systematically Engineering Organizational Change, they will have ensured that managers (the bosses are on board) with the change and able to give input to employees who are doing new work. While employees are personally responsible for developing their new roles, we openly encourage bosses involved in change to be aggressive about giving workers feedback . . . after all, it's the boss' job to direct the play! It is also the boss' job to answer questions . . . and the more comfortable the boss makes employees feel about the new work situation, the more questions he will get!

- **Measurable goals:** We talked in an earlier step about workers needing performance goals for the new or altered roles they were being asked to play. For goals to be useful in letting people know where they are, measurements must be taken and fed back in a timely manner (real-time is best). It does no good to provide quarterly, even monthly, feedback on progress toward goals. Workers in changed organizations need to know how they are doing on at least a weekly basis.

- **Just-in-time assessment** and Training: Another form of feedback can come from the training resources who have helped workers prepare for the new or altered roles. We recommend that trainers who understand the altered work processes and FET make frequent passes through the work force to see how they are doing or to conduct spot assessments or audits of training results (a much more formal role). We have seen organizations put their trainers on call to answer questions from workers in new roles.

- **Customer/peer feedback:** Frequently workers will get feedback from their peers, either verbally or by watching other members of the organization do similar work. We recommend that supervisors encourage workers to talk to their peers to better understand how things are going, for themselves and others. We have seen companies sponsor lunch meetings of small groups of employees to enable conversation among workers who were coming up to speed on new jobs. Sometimes workers get feedback from their customers on how things are going, although we do not encourage it. We want the workers to know what they are doing without having to ask their customers for a grade!

Before we leave this step, it is important to note that formal performance appraisal and salary review systems are rarely of value for job feedback during an organizational change. These formal systems are frequently tied to an annual calendar, and are to be used to give long-term feedback on how the employee is doing overall in what might be a string of altered roles. After an organizational change has been in place for some time, then the formal systems are of great value for giving feedback about how the worker performed in the past review period.

PPI Example 4D: System for monitoring performance

The PPI system for monitoring performance had a number of ingredients: RTB and CTB goals and measures, internal data from the PPI financial system, external data from objective third parties and regularly-scheduled management sessions to analyze the data and determine actions that should be taken for improvement.

After reporting formats had been altered to include both Run-the-Business and Change-the-Business templates, monitoring performance and exchanging feedback occurred at every management meeting and every time a manager looked at his business results. The system for monitoring performance included two different, annual industry surveys administrated by a technical association. One industry survey focused on customer satisfaction and had data on each of the thirteen producers in that industry segment. The second industry survey focused on financial measures like Revenue per FTE/Employee, Return on Capital Employed, and Return on Assets.

The CEO wanted to go beyond traditional monitoring of performance; he chartered what became an annual, organization-wide employee survey that included a number of questions related to RTB/CTB. For example, questions asked about the clarity and understanding of the company vision, critical success factors, business goals, change goals, adequacy of training, five dimensions of job satisfaction, etc.

The survey was designed and administered by a third party who worked with the management team to analyze survey results, make year-to-year comparisons and to develop concrete action plans for organizational improvement. The outside administrator described the results of each year's survey in an organization-wide open meeting of all employees. He was immediately followed at the front of the room by the CEO and members of his management team who detailed the actions that were being taken to improve the organization and the workplace. The action plans were clearly linked to survey results, a linkage that increased the participation in surveys to 70%+ over the years.

OPM NOTE 4D

PPI's performance in managing change was informally monitored and evaluated every time a corporate officer asked how things were going on both Run-the-Business and Change-the-Business.

In-house evaluation of PPI progress in managing change was done by the CEO and the Director of Quality. They frequently stayed on after management meetings to talk over change progress. On some occasion, an executive "who had issues with his part of the organizational change" was asked to stay late as well for coaching and problem solving.

While these after-meeting meetings were almost always positive and supportive of the executive with the issues, Executive Team *members tried hard to "not have issues" with their parts of the organizational change!*

Requirement 4E: Alter and communicate compensation payoffs

Mind-Clearing Example: Imagine an actor who goes on stage for opening night of the new play wearing his old costume and singing his favorite song from the last play. Imagine the Director saying, "Well, your performance is not really what I expected or wanted . . . but here is your paycheck anyway."

Mind-Clearing Example—Or imagine an actor who gets his first paycheck after starting rehearsals for a new play. Imagine the actor complaining to the producer and director that the amount of the check did not match his newly-negotiated compensation contract . . . and then hearing, "We decided not to change paychecks right now for anybody in the theater company. Changing the amounts on the checks would really put a strain on our accountant!

When workers start doing work that is relatively new to them, they need to see and understand how that new work is related to how they get paid. Working people follow the money. We all work for pay. Money counts. Show them where the money is . . . and where the money is not . . . and they will direct themselves toward the money and away from the deficit.

The challenge for the change leader is to compensate employees for the work that matches the new way of doing business . . . and to not compensate for work that no longer aligns with the new way of doing business! The compensation principles that apply in transitioning workers from an old way of working to a new one are as follows:

* Compensation is earned when performance, as defined in the new way of doing business is delivered at the level agreed-to in the agreement with the boss (the organization)

- Continued performance of the old role after change-over to the new way of doing business will not result in any compensation from the firm.

We have found no more difficult job than convincing change leaders and managers alike that the organization must pay for the work needed from employees . . . and not pay for work that is not needed. While this sounds simple enough, it is very difficult to get managers in some companies to act in this emotion-laden area of performance management.

The need to match pay and performance is sometimes easier to see in the case of vendors or contract employees. No capable manager would pay contract employees for doing work that was no longer a part of the current statement of work in the vendor's contract. (Imagine defending yourself to your boss if you did!) And no capable manager would go forward with new vendor contracts and then refuse to pay except under the terms of the old contract.

Unfortunately, it is very common to see change leaders and managers paying workers their regular salaries even though the workers have not yet adopted their new roles in the changed organization. Paying workers even though they do not change their roles sends an immediate signal to these workers and those around them that doing business the new way is not required or desired. So, there are actions that need to be taken to ensure the compensation system "pays off for change" and "doesn't pay off for failure to change." These steps involve mechanically changing the payoff rules in the company's performance management system . . . and then following the rules for compensation with a great deal of discipline.[23]

---

[23]   The idea of paying for work you do want and not paying for work that is not wanted is easier said than done. Don't do anything until you have conferred with your Human Resources Officer and jointly developed a game plan for action with any employee.

Align the payoff rules with the new and altered roles

The idea of payoff rules is simple. We want to have a set of rules or guidelines that tell us what to pay and when to pay it for different performance levels. For a vendor, we have terms in his contract that state that he will be paid after certain specified work has been satisfactorily completed. The specified work is normally listed right in the contract so there is no confusion about what work goes with what pay. In some vendor contracts, we find incentive compensation—extra dollars that the vendor might receive if the work is done in some exceptional way. Normally, the criteria for deciding on the extra incentive compensation are listed in detail.

For employees, such payoff rules are more often implied than written into an explicit contract between worker and employing organization. The payoff rule normally followed by a company is that the worker is due his agreed-to monthly compensation when he satisfactorily performs the work called for in his job (as documented sometimes in a job description). In some companies that offer incentive compensation, additional dollars might be won by the employee by achieving certain goals or targets. Many companies write down these targets at the beginning of the evaluation period (usually a year) so that they can make any incentive compensation calculations needed at the end of the year after work results are available for evaluation.

The change leader's job is to cause the old job description that drove salary to be replaced with the new job description of the altered role that now drives salary. In addition, the change leader must ensure that all "old goals" in the files or paperwork have been replaced by the new goals that go with the altered roles.

This is not rocket science . . . but the details count! If we have thirty workers moving to altered roles and goals, somebody needs to ensure that there are thirty altered job descriptions and sets of goals inserted in the company's files in place of thirty old role descriptions and goal sets. This paperwork change is absolutely necessary so that the company's accountants who ensure that everyone in the company gets the right check written for the right person at the right time can do that accurately.

Follow the payoff rules on a day-to-day basis

Changing the paperwork is a key first step to ensuring that the organization will pay for the performance it wants and not pay for performance it does not want. But the critical ingredient that makes the pay for performance linkage work is the boss. Which boss? Every boss! Every boss in the organization must follow the payoff rules to the letter to ensure that employees all align their behavior with the vision. Every boss must:

- **Coach workers toward performance on the mark:** The boss' job is to ensure that the workers on his watch are moving toward peak performance in altered roles . . . using altered work processes with altered FET . . . to achieve the new way of doing business. The boss' goal should be to win for the company while coaching each employee in how to win for himself.

- **Give real-time feedback for performance off the mark:** When a boss sees performance off the mark (not aligned with the vision), she should give real-time feedback to the worker to give him the chance to get back on track. More coaching might be required to show the worker how to do that or to provide the training needed to get the worker's skills to the desired level.

- **Provide coaching and counseling for performance off the mark:** For workers whose performance is repeatedly off the mark, the boss should provide what we call "counseling" . . . exploring with the employee the reasons why performance does not comply with the direction in the vision . . . or the coaching. The goal would be to assist the worker in the steps needed to get back or track . . . or to consider leaving the organization or his role.

- **Put jobs at risk for those employees consistently off the mark:** If a worker is not willing to perform to the mark, the boss has no choice but to tell the employee that his employment is at risk. That is, the boss says, "You have not demonstrated the kind or level of performance this organization is willing to pay for . . . therefore we are putting you on probation . . ." Most companies already have a policy or procedure for dealing with unsatisfactory performance. In situations like this, the boss should work directly with her Human Resources Department to ensure that her intentions and needs are met within the organization's guidelines.

- **Remove employees who do not comply:** Organizations that want to master change to deal with today's turbulent business environment must be willing to take firm action. Failure to remove someone from the organization who refuses to go along with an organizational change can send a message to other workers that will cripple the organization's future change capability. Our experience is that one removal in an organization is a powerful message that the officially-announced organizational change is truly not optional!

PPI Example 4E: Alter and communicate compensation payoffs

One of the most controversial (at first) aspects of the RTB/CTB method was the compensation policy for managers. The CEO expressed his ideas about compensation philosophy in front of his managers on several occasions. After considerable back-and-forth conversation, the CEO, with the Director of Human Resources, announced the official management compensation policy.

- *The policy treated Run-the-Business performance (i.e., annual business goals) as what managers gave in consideration of their salary.*

- *Managers who exceeded their annual RTB targets received no more compensation above their salaries, a policy rarely used in the chemical industry.*

- The only way managers could earn incentive compensation was by meeting and/or exceeding their annual Change-the-Business targets.

CEO: We were unwavering in applying the Run-the-Business/ Change-the-Business compensation model. Achievement of RTB targets (annual business goals) was required to earn "salary." Achievement of CTB targets (annual change initiatives) was required for any "incentive compensation."

OPM NOTE 4E

A powerful and fundamental factor in motivating the efficient management of change is a very simple one: compensation for change. In a typical company, compensation is based on the manager's organizational level and her performance evaluations. The typical performance evaluation is based on Run-the-Business performance . . . and not on performance in managing change.

Managers who are only evaluated and compensated for Run-the-Business performance are literally paid not to change. In fact, failure to evaluate a manager's performance in CTB is akin to a direct invitation not to be involved with any organizational change.

And in conclusion . . .

The mechanism used to transition actors from one play to the next is the "contract" that formalizes the agreement between actor and theater company to work together, under certain terms, in the next play.

For successful organizational change, employees must be under agreement to perform to the vision of the new way of doing business. In addition, all employees must be under contract for the process of transitioning to this vision, a period of time during which they will be:

- Performing their normal, routine duties for the current way of operating, and
- Performing the change work necessary to transition to the company's new way of doing business.

Failing to alter the performance management system to align with the desired new way of doing business while expecting successful organizational change is akin to expecting the performance of a new play from actors who are still under exclusive contract for performing the old play!

For successful organization change, there must be physical alteration of the business system that the organization uses to direct and reinforce the performance of its managers and employees. This performance management system is the organization's mechanism for procuring, directing, and retaining the kind of performance it needs. This performance management system must be altered in order to (1) reinforce the transition to the new organizational future and (2) to dis-incentivize failure to transition to the new future

OPM implementation will require many changes when it comes to the work of individual project managers and project team members, as well as program and portfolio managers. Executive management will also have to look at strategic planning in a new light. PMI's growing number of certifications will help an organization change the way its professionals are doing their work. Performance management can be better enabled by preparing people for certification exams.

These professional certifications will make it easier for project, program, and portfolio managers to accept their new roles. The Enterprise PMO will be responsible for developing training programs as well as performance management systems. Often looked at as an overhead function and often abandoned because of this negative image, it becomes quite clear, as we look at OPM implementation, how critical the Enterprise PMO will be to any organization desiring to carry out real change through effective Organizational Project Management.

Chapter Eight

Use Project Management to Guide Change

Mind-Clearing Example—Imagine the Director who has identified the new play and the opening date but who has developed no action plans for the weeks of work needed to transition from the old play to the new.

Imagine the theater company not knowing when final role assignments were to be made, when new costumes were to be fitted, when rehearsals were to be held, when the sets needed to be completed, when the stage rigging would be tested, and so on.

When asked about the schedule for key transition events, the Director answers, "I'm busy worrying about the long-term future of our theater company . . . and I certainly don't have time to work through the kinds of details you all seem to be so worried about!"

The vision of the new way of doing business clearly provides guidance for organizational change. But time spent gazing into a future (that will always have some mystery in it) can be wasted if immediate and obvious actions at hand cannot be taken. Requirement five of organizational change is to construct and fully communicate project action plans and schedules for change work for each week or month of the organizational change. Organization members need specific plans and schedules that detail the week-by-week change work they must complete to get to the new way of doing business. Workers must know what change work to do "on Monday morning" (and every other Monday morning) . . . along with their "day jobs," the current work they are already doing.

For minor organizational change, the amount of change work to be done may be quite small, involving only a few workers or work processes. But for major organizational changes that will involve many workers (maybe thousands) and several work processes (maybe dozens), the amount of change work that must be completed can be huge and overwhelming! Without at least weekly scheduling of specific change work to do, the organizational change effort will just bog down as organization members focus their time and energy on their obvious day jobs of producing products and services.

Manage organizational change like a project

We have used the word "project" several times in this book . . . but not with the degree of emphasis needed for effective organizational change. We mean to treat change work as a real project that has an identity as well as a manager with the authority and resources needed to get it finished. We mean that change work must be managed with the discipline of project management . . . a specialized and well-developed management field that deals with getting unique work done in an organized, systematic manner . . . on target, on time and on budget. In this chapter on using project management for change, we unabashedly state that change work must be subjected to disciplined management . . . and the closest developed capability to what is needed here is project management.

The master schedule shows the overall timetable and sequence of activities associated with organizational change. Companies that have mastered change put the Project Charter and the master schedule as the first steps and use them to guide change work all the way from vision development to the final celebration of success.

The general sequence of work to be managed in an organizational change project is as follows:

1. **Chartering the organizational change as a project:** The executive who is commissioning the organizational change should appoint a formal project manager and give this professional the initial assignment of developing the formal charter for the change

project. The Project Charter is the executive's and project manager's concise statement of the intent, goals, scope, change budget, limits of and responsibilities for the organizational change.

2. **Development, approval and communication of the master schedule:** The project manager sketches the beginning and desired end points of the organizational change, develops the work breakdown structure and task list,[24] creates the first high-level master schedule, and seeks schedule approval by the executive in charge of the change.

> **The Shock and Awe of Organizational Change**
>
> *The first cut at a master schedule can produce big surprises for organizational leadership—when the first schedule reveals the realities of the upcoming change. The draft schedule shows the time and people involved, the number of steps that must be taken and managed, the resources that will be required, etc. In short, senior management can see for the first time all the change work that must be completed while the organization continues to do its "day job" of serving customers.*

3. **Development of the vision and the case for organizational change:** The change leader, or Program Manager, launches those activities needed to develop the vision of the new way of doing business in some detail as well as the case for change.

4. **Initial communication of the vision and case for change:** The change leader begins the communication process designed to

---

[24] The Work breakdown structure (WBS) is the technical term that project managers use to describe all the work that will need to be done to finish the organizational change, on target, on time, and on budget. The WBS, a functional decomposition of a project's deliverables, will help, through the subsequent definition of the project tasks, to organize the work to be done in a logical order that can be resourced and managed.

give the organization a heads up to changes that are to be made along with the reasons for those changes.

5. **Identification of change work, that is, the alterations that will need to be made**: The change leader or Program Manager names Project Teams to identify needed alterations in

   o Work processes
   o Facilities, Equipment, Technology (FET)
   o Performance management system (e.g., worker roles, training, etc.)

6. **Development and communication of a detailed master schedule:** A detailed master schedule is created to show the calendar for completing all needed Change Work.

7. **Alteration of worker roles:** the change leader authorizes bosses to conduct one-on-one contracting with workers for

   o **Starting a new way of working** at the targeted, change-over time
   o **Continuing to perform work** as it is currently done until change-over
   o **Completing the change work** required for change-over (e.g., participating in training, new role development, new equipment break-in, etc.)

8. **Conducting change work:** Many consider this step as the heart of organizational change, where existing work processes are studied, re-designed, and then altered to fit the change vision; where FET is analyzed and actions taken to modify it or to buy and install new FET; and where roles are altered and training delivered, and so on. This step alone can take weeks to months of hard work for some organization members while other members are uninvolved, continuing to conduct today's business as usual . . . until that first training class appears on their schedules.

9. **Verifying all change work:** The change leader ensures all the needed change work has been done, including alteration of work

processes, FET, and roles . . . and that tests have been conducted to ensure that all needed alterations have been adequately made.

10. **Changing over to the new way of doing business:** At the specific time(s) the various parts of the organization make the switch from doing work the old way to doing work the new way. With OPM, this will begin to happen as prototypes of work processes and systems are completed and deemed successful.

11. **Break-in (or learning curve phase) and stabilization:** The change leader aggressively leads during the first few weeks/months of working the new way, during which the organization continues to learn and make further refinements to work processes, FET, and worker roles to achieve the desired way of doing business.

Leadership for the change Initiative

Mind-Clearing Example—Imagine the director telling her investors in the new play that she decided not to be responsible or accountable for the preparation for the new play. Imagine the investors' reactions when she says, "I really hate all this transition and preparation stuff; I'm going to let my assistants be responsible for it!"

A significant organizational change needs leadership . . . and lots of it! While the titles of leaders may vary by organization, we believe the following leadership roles are needed for effective and efficient organizational change:

- *CEO: The CEO is ultimately responsible and accountable for the Change-the-Business Management Systems and any and all changes to the way the organization does business. The CEO's leadership is required to give direction and authority to organizational changes. The Change Leader and the Manager of the Program Management Office (PMO) would assist the CEO and shoulder the majority of the Change Management work.*

- **Change Leader:** *The Executive who is in charge of those parts of the organization impacted by the change is the Change Leader (or the Executive in Charge). For example, a major change in Operations should be led by the COO, under the direct leadership of the CEO. The Change Leader would be assisted by the Program or Project Manager and the Manager of the Program Management Office.*

- **Project Manager:** *Depending on the size and scope of the change and the number of needed projects, this primary role could be called the Program Manager of the Change. This key leader reports to the Change Leader and is the prime move of the change on a day-to-day business. Multiple Project Managers may report to the Program Manager, playing the same day-to-day leadership role on projects with more narrow scope.*

  A big step in the right direction for managing change will be to encourage all project management professionals to pursue the various certifications offered by the Project Management Institute. As more and more professionals achieve certification, they will be less tolerant of less than adequate approaches for managing projects and programs.

- **Manager of the Program Management Office (PMO):** *The Manager of the PMO is responsible for resourcing the five major functional areas of OPM (i.e., the Change-the-Business Management System). All major changes initiatives going on in an organization at any point in time should be tracked and resourced by the PMO. This manager may report to the CEO or to another senior Executive. The Manager of the PMO is not in the primary management chain of command that begins with the CEO to the COO to other line managers who are responsible for production and people.*

While the boss cannot escape the ultimate accountability for organizational change and for the management of the change project, she can use able assistants to help. These assistants can be most helpful if they have project management skills and experience. In fact, starting a big organizational change effort without an experienced Project

Management Professional (PMP) in a key role is an almost certain recipe for a change that will be . . . off target, off schedule, and way over budget.

It is still interesting to us as consultants to see managers who would not dare tackle the construction of a major capital asset without the assistance of a professional-level, project management firm . . . move forward with a multi-million dollar organizational change without an experienced project manager somewhere in the loop!

> **Mind-Clearing Example—Imagine** the Director who tells his investors that he is firmly in control of the transition to the new play. "Why," he says, "I have found a management intern who is pretty darn smart, and I have turned the transition management over to her! I am involved, of course. I have lunch with her every week or so, and we go over things."

The Project Manager who will be put in charge of an organizational change must know all the "mechanical stuff" about project management: building and documenting the project plan, ensuring that all required resources are assigned to the project and clearly tasked, monitoring and reporting on project performance (i.e., schedule, cost, quality and risk), managing project interdependencies, and so on.[25]

But in addition, the following skills, experiences, and sensitivities are critical for the success of the Project Manager:

- **Cognizance of "Run-the-Business, Change-the-Business"**
  Organizational change does not occur in a vacuum but while the current business is running at full speed. The Project manager must be able to take into account his organization's Run-the-Business situation and flex change project planning to ensure that there will be enough executive focus and energy to keep the change initiative moving. For example, the project manager who insists that the executive team meet this week for

---

[25]

the regular monthly change status report while the executives are fighting a major quality issue that has just arisen is going to lose credibility and stature by being just plain dumb.

- **Knowledge of the company and the industry in which it competes**
  In many mature industries, the differences between success and failure are very small and hard to see or appreciate by anyone who does not have "the business in his bones." A mechanical project manager with no touch or feel for the business or for her organization cannot do the change job well enough for success. While the project manager cannot know everything about the business, he or she needs to be able to discern the subject matter expertise that needs to be added to the project. The project manager does not need to know everything, but does need to know where to find everything that needs knowing.

- **Willingness to call a spade a spade in front of the CEO and her executive team**
  Regardless of the potential bounty of an organizational change, sailing will not always be smooth. Managers are, after all, paid to be biased in the direction of the functions they represent, and they are not always eager to make needed changes in their units when maybe it's the other guy's unit that should be making changes. So there will be issues and conflicts that can only be resolved around the executive table with the CEO in charge. The project manager, as the person who has to put issues on that table, cannot be hesitant or shy about pointing out risks or about escalating issues to the top of the organization.

- **Excellent interpersonal and communication skills**
  We have all heard the saying that "if you cannot measure it, you cannot manage it." For organizational change we can add the saying "if you cannot say it, you cannot lead it." The Project manager must be able to communicate clearly and intelligently, and be able to describe the desired organizational change and what must be done to successfully complete the change. Having

good interpersonal skills will also be essential to lead organization members to do the right things at the right time.

After reading this section of the chapter, some readers have said that we are asking for Superman (or woman) to be the project manager of an organizational change. Are we? Changing the direction of a multi-billion dollar organization with a few thousand employees scattered over a hundred or so countries is not a task for just anyone. But a solid manager with the qualifications we have talked about who uses the road map in this book can competently lead change initiatives.

This chapter is all about getting in control of the needed change work so that the desired organizational change can be made . . . on target, on time, and on budget. Getting change work under control requires a project management mindset, a robust planning and scheduling method, critical path planning, valid work breakdown structures and task list, weekly schedules, and several one-on-one meetings with the workers involved in the change. And as a critical overlay, getting change work under control means explicit and disciplined risk management.

Figure 8.1: Risks to manage in an organization change

Managing risks in an organizational change project[26]

Taking an organization that is doing work one way and changing that organization to work in another way is not an easy or certain exercise. Therefore, a critical project management discipline is risk management. The size of the risks in an organizational change can be anything from a few thousand dollars for small changes to hundreds of millions for potential disruption to a large organization or to its customers.

There are many risks along the way . . . risks that must be explicitly and aggressively managed for the change to be successfully completed. We have identified three categories of risks that must be managed during the process of organizational change:

- **Technical risk:** the chance that various parts of the organization and its moving parts will not work the way they were planned to work. Technical failure could be needed equipment that does not work as intended (or advertised), work processes that do not achieve the desired result, and so on. Imagine the props in a new theater production functioning so poorly that attention is diverted away from the actors!

- **Organizational risk:** the chance organization members will not accept the change to the new way of doing business. Imagine actors on the stage for a new performance who clearly do not have their hearts in the play and who give only a half-hearted performance!

- **Business risk:** the chance the costly-to-implement organizational change will not pay off in dollars and cents. Failure to gain a favorable business outcome could be caused by a number of factors, from poor design of the change (e.g., presenting a new way of working that customers do not like) to flawed implementation (causing even a good organizational change design to feel wrong to customers and employees alike). Imagine a

---

26   Change Is the Rule: Practical Action for Change: On Target, On Time, On Budget, Winford E Holland, Dearborn Press, Chicago: 2000.

We doubt that there is an experienced worker anywhere who has not seen an organizational change that either did not work from a technical point of view, was not used, or, if used, made no money for the organization. Comprehensive risk management is a tall order for many of today's organizations that generally focus on technical risk mitigation alone while organizational and business risks are left to chance. The organizational change message is very clear—plan to manage all three kinds of risks effectively—or keep your present way of doing business in play. Moving ahead toward a new way of doing business without managing all three risks is a certain recipe for organizational disruption and even disaster.

Identify and verify deadly assumptions that will disable project management

The idea of using project management as a disciplined way of guiding a transition to a new way of doing business is hard to dismiss. But for line managers who spend their time running the daily business, the whole idea of project management is just what it is . . . an idea. Project management as a discipline is very different way of managing than most managers have experienced.

Project management is needed because a change to a new way of doing business is a "unique deliverable," exactly what project management produces. In a transition, the organization needs to be operating in the new way on target, on time and on budget, requiring planning and control skills not normally found in line managers. We have seen the most success when experienced project managers were brought in to change projects to guide and keep track of the many steps that will need to be taken before the organizational change is complete. Unfortunately many managers do not appreciate the value of disciplined Project Management. "We can do without it," some say. "We have been getting along without it, haven't we?" Yes you have, and that's a critical reason most change initiatives don't work!

Step	Change-Blocking Assumption	Disabling Behavior	Proven Consequences
Requirement Five: Project Management of Change Projects	People manage themselves every day, and they will manage themselves through this change	Missing or inadequate day-to-day plans and schedules for organized preparation and implementation of change	• Uneven implementation • False starts • Inconsistent results

Change leaders can spot the likely presence of deadly assumptions through conversations heard about what needs to be done to get the change completed or to get project management into place. Hearing the suggestion to "just let people move at their own pace; you know, some of us are busier than others" calls for the change leader to surface deadly assumptions and to dispel them in any way possible, starting with the proven consequences in the table above.

Take these Action Steps to Complete Requirement Five: Use Project Management for Implementing Change

Now we are on to the hard work of managing the overall organizational change with the following five steps: Skip a step and expect expensive delays.

Action steps for Project Management

- 5A: Develop Project Charter for executive approval
- 5B: Set and communicate master schedule
- 5C: Use week-at-a-time implementation scheduling with one-on-one assignments
- 5D: Regularly check transition progress and re-schedule as needed
- 5E: Confirm, stabilize and celebrate the completed transition to the new way of doing business

Requirement 5A: Develop Project Charter for executive approval

Mind-Clearing Example—Imagine a Director who makes an oral presentation to the Producer and investors about his desire to put on a new play to replace the current one. When asked about the details of the new play or about a document that describes his proposed project, the Director says, "I haven't had time to work out any details . . . and I sure don't want to waste any time writing stuff down. I just want to get your approval for the play so I can get started. As we work through the details, perhaps I can have my assistant brief you if you like."

The trick is to look at all the needed change work as a project. The project must be managed to get the needed change work done in an organized and systematic way—while the organization carries on with its current way of doing business: making products, serving clients, seeing patients, etc. The first step, and some would say, the single most important step for getting the needed change work done is to develop a Project Charter containing basic information that can be used to steer the entire change project.

The Project Charter is a formal document that describes the purpose or intent of the organizational change, the way the change project will be structured and how it will be successfully implemented. A fully functional Project Charter will describe:

- What we are trying to do with the change: vision, scope, objectives and deliverables
- How we will accomplish the change: approach, methods, milestones, budgets, resources
- Who will be involved in the change: stakeholders, executive in charge, project manager roles and responsibilities

The Project Charter should be first drafted by the project manager after extensive conversations with the executives who believe the change is necessary. The project manager may not get the needed information from simple conversations so he or she should be prepared to ask prepared questions to obtain needed information. Frequently organizational changes are ignited by a study, a task force report, or an executive retreat. In that case, the project manager should ask for any materials that came from such formal efforts: studies, minutes of meetings, wall charts or whatever was used to record the thinking behind the organizational change.

The components of the Project Charter

Before we dive into the nuts and bolts of the Project Charter, let's review a bit. An organization's executive leadership has deliberated and concluded that their organization needs to change some aspects of the way it is doing business. While there is executive direction (perhaps, a high-level vision) and intent, there is not as yet any organized way of making that change happen, hopefully, on target, on time, and on budget. If the CEO shouted to the entire organization, "Here is our high level vision for the future . . . let's get started tomorrow," most of us would likely predict a certain amount of paralysis mixed with pandemonium as the order of the day.

This chapter, this part of the successful organizational change process, is designed to explain how to take a high-level vision and develop action plans that will enable the change to be made in an organized and predictable way. That is a tall order in anybody's book. The Project Charter serves as the foundation for the organizational change and should contain the following high-level information:

1. The **purpose** and/or intent of the change
2. **The specific objectives** and deliverables of the change
3. **The scope of the change**, what parts of the organization will be affected
4. **The change approach** including high level phases and milestones
5. **The implementation steps** for the change
6. **The stakeholders** in the change
7. **The leadership roles** and responsibilities in the change
8. **The preliminary budget** for the change

The list above is not a strict formula, and change leaders can get by with a few more or a few less components, as long as the entries to those sections are valid. Better yet, templates for project charters are available for download from the web. While the templates are different, some provide almost fool proof instructions for completing them. But caution is needed.

Beware of the holes in any template

Most of the sections of a Project Charter can be filled in with the information at hand. There are no right or wrong answers to sections like "goals, scope or stakeholders." But there are right or wrong (valid or invalid) answers to the following sections:

- The approach,
- Implementation steps, and
- Leadership roles and responsibilities.

The purpose of this book is to give valid information for those three sections. Failure to use valid information will produce a Charter that is likely to lead to an unsuccessful organizational change. Fore-warned is fore-armed!

The Project or Program Manager should produce the draft of the Project Charter. But input for the draft must come from a set (or team) of organization members that have the competencies in the Figure below (See Section 4C). As you can see in the Figure, the absence of only one of the competencies will have a dramatic effect on the quality of the Project Charter.

Project Management Competence?	Industry and Company Expertise?	Competence in Organizational Mechanics?	Result: A Project Charter that is:
Yes	Yes	Yes →	• Workable • Sound • A solid base
No	Yes	Yes →	• In disarray • Confusing • "Stop and Start"
Yes	No	Yes →	• Naive • Simplistic • Invalid
Yes	Yes	No →	• Incomplete • Unworkable • Ineffective

Figure 8.2: Consequences of a Missing Competence

The change approach and implementation steps

This part of the Charter is critical because it is where the rubber meets the road for organizational change. In this section of the Charter, the change leader or the project manager describes the approach (i.e., change project phases) and the implementation steps to be used to complete the project. Once the Charter is approved by top management, the project manager is bound to (or guided by) the approved steps that become the recipe for the change. A summary of the action steps we have covered is shown in condensed form in the Appendix: Task List for successful organizational change.

The figure below is a schematic of the integration of project management phases and change management steps. The phases of the project are shown across the top of the figure while the change management components are shown in the first column. Reading across each row, you can see the elements of the work breakdown structure we have described in earlier parts of the book.

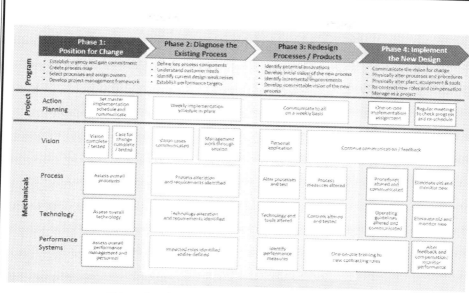

Figure 8.3: Integration of Project Management
and Change Engineering

The purpose of the figure is to show how integration works from what might be called an academic point of view. The figure answers many questions that have been raised in the change management community about the way project management and change management work together.

The Last Change to Avoid Certain Failure of Organizational Change

One last time, the approach and implementation steps that go into the Project Charter and that are approved by the top executive will set the course for the organizational change. If the Charter contains invalid steps, change goals will not be met. It is as simple as that . . . and frequently it is the project manager who gets egg on his face. If the Charter leaves out critical steps, the project manager is in for an uphill battle to insert a missing step after the change initiative gets rolling.

Get it right. The contents of this book are designed to be the right stuff, the right content for the approach and implementation steps. Successful organizational change is now within your reach.

The organization of the project

The leadership roles and responsibilities for the change project are also critical in the Charter. The way the change leadership is organized can make the difference between success and failure of the organizational change. Three leadership configurations are shown below; one will make change possible while the other two will likely stop or dilute any change efforts.

The logical place to start, and where many other explanations stop, is the pure project organization as shown in figure 8.4. This figure shows how multiple projects might fit under a master Project or Program Manager. This figure is clearly a valuable picture of a part of the organization needed for project success. But any change project is going to be worked while the organization carries on with its regular business of producing today's products and serving today's customers. How will this pure project organizational design work? Is the organizational change to be firmly anchored in thin air?

The next figure shows the connection between the Change-the-Business structure and the Run-the-Business organization. Figure 8.5 shows the Program Manager connected to the day-to-day organizational structure for Running the business. This figure is a revelation to many as they see for the first time that change initiatives and/or programs are real parts of the formal organization and its day-to-day operation.

There are two important aspects of Figure 8.5 to note. First note that the program manager, to whom all change projects report, has a dotted line relationship directly to the CEO with a solid line relationship to what is called a Steering Committee. Such an arrangement frequently has a Steering Committee made up of senior functional managers who report to the CEO on a day-to-day basis.

Second, while serving on the steering committee, each Senior Manager is expected to "wear his company or enterprise leadership hat" objectively . . . rather than being a representative of his unit only. This looks good but there is still a problem because there is a solid line connection between the Steering Committee and the Program Manager, meaning that those Steering Committee members have ultimate control over change projects that will surely involve their own organizations. Such an arrangement will likely result in informal political bargaining among Committee members that can keep a change effort from have the full desired effect (or even put the success of the change initiative in jeopardy)!

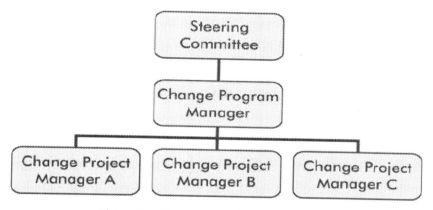

Figure 8.4: The pure project organization

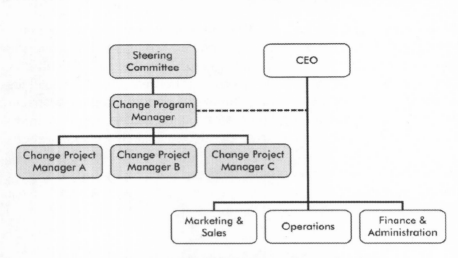

**Figure 8.5: The CTB Organization connected to the
Run-the-Business Organization**

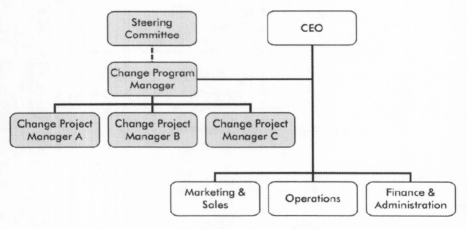

Figure 8.6: The CTB Organization connected directly to the CEO

Figure 8.6 also shows the project organization connected to the day-to-day organizational structure for running the business, but in this organizational design, the Steering Committee can provide input to the program manager but they cannot make a final decision about a change issue. That responsibility rests with the CEO only . . . as shown by the solid line between CEO and the Program Manager. In practice, once everybody understands the lay of the land from a structure point of view, the Steering Committee usually plays nice and, as a result, the Program Manager does not have to take too many issues to the CEO for resolution. However, with this arrangement, the threat of the CEO becoming involved in an issue is a constant reminder for the steering committee to always wear their organizational hats rather than individually wearing their functional hats.

Executive approval of the Project Charter

We use the contents of the Project Charter as well as the contents of any planning notes or documents to construct a presentation for executive approval. Our presentation is designed to say or convey several key messages:

- **We heard your intent** and that is what is guiding our change project The idea here is to be sure that the executive hears his words coming back to him or her. The executive should be able to say, "Yep, that is what I was talking about!" As soon as the executive recognizes the project manager's alignment, the project manager's credibility goes up.

- **We have done our homework.** The executive should hear that the project manager has done extensive analysis and planning for the organizational change. A slide that shows who has been consulted in the organization about what subject will do wonders to build credibility if, and only if, the names on the list are the "A" players in the organization.

- **We are ready to rock and roll.** The executive should hear that the project manager has covered all the bases to ensure that stakeholders know what is going on, what their stake is, and what they will be responsible for completing.

- **We do have some issues.** The issues confronting the project managers can be listed at this time along with a suggested solution for each issue. It is critical not to show an issue that does not have one or more solutions ready to be approved. If a presented issue does not have an immediate solution in the room, the project manager should not leave the room until there is agreement on who and how the issue will be resolved as well as whether or not the project must wait for issue resolution or can start in anticipation of a successful resolution of the issue.

- **Just say the word, Boss.** The executive should feel that the project manager is "straining at the leash" to get started. The executive should see, hear and feel the project manager's alignment with the intent of the change, her passion, her readiness, and her confidence that the change is under good control.

We could tell horror stories here about project managers who translate the executive's words into "change-speak," using change management and behavioral science terms that mean nothing to the executive but do cause him to question the competence of the Project Manager. The presentation to executives that seeks approval of the Project Charter is a "big deal" pitch; failure in this presentation may have many negative consequences including slowing the organizational change, confusing those in the presentation, and/or costing the project managers her job.

> *PPI Example 5A: Develop Project Charter for executive approval*
>
> *The Project Charter for the PPI performance improvement initiative took shape over the first few weeks of the new CEO's tenure. The Director of Quality faithfully kept a running Charter document as various parts of the RTB /CTB took shape. With the running notes, the CEO and his direct reports were able to review and remember important points and decisions made by the Executive Team.*
>
> *Even CEOs have a boss, in this case, in the form of a Division CEO from headquarters. While the PPI CEO was in almost daily phone contact with his boss, the CEO began to plan for his boss' first visit to the PPI offices and plants. The CEO and the Director*

of Quality worked on the "CTB charter" while the CEO and CFO worked to prepare the Run-the-Business briefing.

The CEO's boss called the PPI CEO the day before this first visit and said, "I won't have much time tomorrow, so all I want to hear is two things: (1) how you are going to keep the profit we have, and (2) how you are going to get profitability up?"

The PPI CEO reduced his slide deck to two slides: the first slide entitled Run-the-Business listed the top ten actions there were currently engaged in to maintain the current profit level, and the second slide showed the vision statement at the top of the page along with a listing of five performance improvement projects (i.e., Perfect Service) that were up and running along with each project's target impact on PPI. The two slides went over well, and they were the foundation of a very good conversation between the two leaders, the first of many.

OPM NOTE 5A

In this case where PPI was doing two things at once (i.e., striving for Perfect Service and implementing a new way of doing the business of change), the project was formed around the Perfect Service initiative. Had there been only one change being attempted (i.e., the change to OPM /CTB), the project structure and schedule would have been around OPM.

Having seen OPM /CTB implementation attempted both ways (i.e., OPM alone or with another change), we believe it to be far easier to implement OPM while another major change is going on (i.e., like the PPI case).

Requirement 5B: Set and Communicate the Master Schedule for Change Work

> *Mind-Clearing Example—Imagine a Director who has no master schedule for the work to be done to transition her theater company from the old play to the new one.*
>
> *When asked about the calendar dates for key transition events (like contracting with actors, fitting costumes, conducting rehearsals, etc.), she answers, "Well, the situation is much too fluid to put things down on a calendar. We'll just have to wait to see how things work out, won't we?"*

In the first four requirements for organizational change, we have identified much of the change work that will need to be done:

- We have a vision that needs to be detailed and communicated to the organization,
- We have work process alterations that need to be made,
- We have alterations to make in the organization's FET to fit altered processes
- We have individual worker role alterations to make and contracting sessions to conduct, and so on.

As we have said before, the trick is to look at all the needed change work as a project. The project must be managed to get the needed change work done in an organized and systematic way—while the organization carries on with its current way of doing business, making products, serving customers, etc. The single most important tool for getting the needed change work done is the master schedule . . . which is driven by the work breakdown structure and task list.

Work Breakdown Structure

This book has been about detailing the steps in the work breakdown structure for an organization change. The previous chapters provided the "nuts and bolts" actions associated with the four major work elements.

Now it is up to the project manager to put those nut-and-bolt actions into a logical, master schedule that takes into account the realities of the

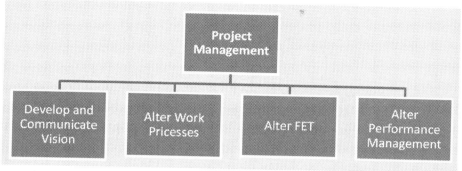

Figure 8.7: Work breakdown structure for project management

organization that is to be changed. The actual schedule that will be constructed will not be exactly linear because of the need to accommodate organization dates, other major initiatives, and the priorities associated with the current business.

Critical attributes of the Master Schedule

Regardless of the magnitude of the organizational change, the master schedule should have the following attributes to be a sound base for managing an organizational change:

- **Comprehensiveness:** the master schedule must include all moving parts of the organizational change . . . not just the most visible parts (like the purchase and installation of new FET). Work process and worker role alterations, contracting sessions, training classes, project management, and quality management tasks . . . all must go on the master schedule!

- **Realism:** We have seen timetables for organizational change that were about as unrealistic as driving your SUV to the moon. Change work takes time and energy . . . and must fit into or around the already busy schedules of the workers. Realistic time estimates for completing the different kinds of change work must be developed . . . and then folded together if the change is to have any chance of being completed on target, on time, and on budget.

- **Business fit:** As we have said before, organizations do change work while they continue to do the organization's current work. Scheduling change work must take the schedule of current work into account if the schedule is to be realistic. For example, scheduling work process alterations for an accounting organization while they are in the thick of preparing tax returns for a March 15 deadline is courting a schedule disaster! On the other hand, the master schedule must also take into account the realities of the needed change. If the organization must have a change in place by a certain date to maintain its level of profitability, that reality must be dealt with in the schedule.

- **Critical path schedule:** This kind of schedule shows what change work must be done in what order so that all the change work has the most time-efficient flow. For example, imagine trying to train employees on new equipment that has not yet arrived!

The critical path method is a key discipline within project management and is an absolute requirement for projects that have more than a handful of change work steps. PMI defines the Critical Path as the sequence of activities that represents the longest path through a project, which therefore determines the shortest possible duration.

When we finish explaining master scheduling to our change management clients, we frequently hear an attitude of, "Oh no! Do we really have to do all this detailed planning and scheduling work?" The simple answer is, "Only if you want to have a chance at bringing in your organization change on target, on time, and on budget!" As we have said before, change management is not rocket science but it is engineering—disciplined, detailed hard work! And using a detailed master schedule is a requirement for successful organizational change!

Integrating project management and change management to set the master schedule

Building a master schedule these days starts with the selection of the project management software that will be used to schedule and manage the project. If you have a skilled project manager, odds are he or she already has experience in such project management packages. You may also be able to count on your organization's Information Technology Department to provide you with the needed software package and maybe even somebody to run it for you.

As a word of warning, our experience has been that many organizations elect to use project management software that is much more powerful (and therefore much more complex) than needed. Microsoft Project, in its later versions, has more than enough functionality for even a major organizational change. Other project management software tools are equally effective.

The high-level master schedule can be developed around the change sequence shown earlier in this chapter. The detailed master schedule can be completed after the change leader has a feel for the needed alterations. Input for developing the master schedule can come directly from the lists of needed alterations discussed during the previous chapters on alterations.

1. The vision (the detailed version as described in Chapter Four)
2. Work process alterations (as described in Chapter Five)
3. FET alterations (as described in Chapter Six)
4. Performance system alterations (as described in Chapter Seven)

While a project scheduler might be able to make the first pass at getting these lists of needed alterations into the project management software, it is the ultimate responsibility of the project manager to sit down with that list of activities and turn it into a schedule. We have found this task to work better if the project manager and the scheduler also have the time and energy of some of the people who produced the lists of project alterations. Their input will be invaluable in identifying the three critical parameters needed for a critical path schedule: the sequence of alteration steps, the estimated time to make those alterations, and the staffing required to make the alterations.

Theory aside, organization members need to see answers to questions like, "What do we do on Monday morning? Is the work process training scheduled for this week or next week? And is that "training on the system" or "training on work processes using the system?" When is the new FET going to be available on workers' desk tops, and so on. That's where the master schedule comes in, showing the overall flow of change work that must be done as well as the particular tasks to be completed by workers at each level and in each department.

Odds are that multiple rounds of scheduling might need to occur before the change leader settles on the master schedule she wants to communicate. For example, one round of scheduling might be made using the desired target date for change-over to the new work. This will need to be done first if the change leader has named a desired timeframe during the development of the vision. This step frequently shows that "you can't get there from here" as the old saying goes . . . meaning that all the needed change work may not be possible before the desired new work date.

The second round of scheduling might start with the current date to calculate the projected finish of the change effort. The outcome of this round gives direct feedback on the realism of the original desired change-over date. The change leader can re-work the scheduling process as needed, adjusting time estimates where possible to get a master schedule she and the organization can live with.

Communicating the Master Schedule

The change leader must communicate the master schedule (Figure 8.8) to the key managers of the organization who must be cognizant of the change so that they are prepared to lead their department's share of the change work and to shift to the new work at the targeted change-over date. Since the master schedule will contain a lot of detail (given, of course, the magnitude of the change), all of the organization's managers don't need to see it all; they just need the parts that involve them and their units.

The only practical means for communicating the master schedule to the managers in an already-busy organization is with a face-to-face meeting with them. Until then, the master schedule is just another email attachment or floating piece of paper! It may be tough to schedule those implementation meetings, but that's where the CEO and the Change Leader come in!

The change leader must also create the conditions under which the master schedule will be heard as official notification of actions that must be taken by the involved managers in the organization. If organization member see the master schedule as for your information only (FYI) or nice to know information, they clearly will not be positioned to contribute to an organizational change . . . on target, on time, and on budget.

Developing the change budget

Organizations that have mastered change can not only bring in a change on target and on time but on budget. The logical exercise that goes on with the master scheduling process is project costing. Experienced change leaders know that changing an organization takes real money out of pocket just like building a house takes money. The elements of an organizational change that cost the most money are frequently associated with alterations or new FET. However, other alterations also take money. Listed below are some of those parts of a major organizational change that generate costs for the project budget.

- Alteration of FET including costs of Engineering and Construction vendors and the disposition costs of old FET
- Alteration of work processes and writing procedures requiring overtime or professional services fees

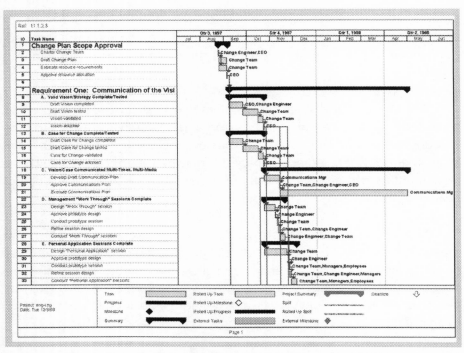

Figure 8.8: Sample of a master schedule on MS Project

- Alteration of worker roles including training costs, new uniforms, possible salary adjustments, etc.
- Development of the Vision, frequently requiring professional fees for consultants, market research, benchmarking, etc.
- Addition of extra personnel to "work the change" including contract programmers for software applications development/ modification, Project Management and/or Change Management specialists to support the work of the change leader and the organization's managers.

The idea is to get to a sound estimate of the cost of organizational change by estimating the costs of the pieces of organizational change. We have used two different approaches that work reasonably well for getting at the costs of organizational change. The first approach might be called the Proposal Approach. In this Approach, the change leaders asks that specific effort and cost proposals be prepared for each identified part of the organizational change as it is planned. Over time an organization can build up a history of change project costs that will be useful for such proposals.

The second approach might be called the business plan approach that calls for the change leader to look at the organizational change as the start-up of a new business. Business people who have approached a bank about a loan for a new business quickly find out that they need a pretty thorough business plan to convince the banker that their dollars will be well used. A convincing business plan shows the structure of the desired new business, the vision, the business steps, and the revenues that can be expected.

In addition the plan must show all the important moving parts that will ensure the Vision is reached. The business plan will need to identify all the actions and assets needed to reach the Vision and the total costs that will be required. We have asked numerous clients to prepare a business plan for change as a part of change management. Results have varied from consistently good business plans from some companies to mediocre plans at best from others. One clear positive result for requiring the business plan, however, is that the requirement forces the changing organization into a mindset that explicitly recognizes the financial costs of change.

Beyond these two approaches, we do have one last resort method to use in the absence of any organized change budgeting. We usually recommend the simple rule of thumb: determine the costs of the new or altered FET and at least double that figure to get an order of magnitude of the total costs that will be incurred in the change project.

Few companies today will launch a major capital expenditure project without a time schedule or cost budget . . . but it is quite common for organizations to undertake a major organizational change with neither, except for those parts of the change that involve a construction project for some of the visible FET. Organizations that want to master change must treat scheduling and budgeting for change just as seriously as they treat budgets and schedules for the normal work of the organization such as making and selling products/services for a profit.

PPI Example 5B: Set and Communicate the Master Schedule for Change Work

PPI had master schedules at two levels. A master schedule was developed and kept current at the senior management level. This schedule showed both the RTB/CTB schedule for the year and included the CTB projects as line items. This master schedule was maintained by the Director of Quality and the CEO, and was used at management meetings of the organization that managed change, as well as at meetings of the CEO and his executive team.

Master schedules were also kept at the project level for the changes being worked for the year. The project manager of each project was responsible for his master schedule, sometimes aided by the Director of Quality and his small staff. The formality of the project-level schedules varied in the degree of detail with the complexity of the change project; the more moving parts, the more formal and detailed the schedule.

OPM NOTE 5B

The Director of Quality (i.e., the nominal Head of the PMO) experimented with several ways of ensuring that project schedules for the "Perfect Service" initiatives were accurate and visible. One technique that worked was to have project schedules on the wall of the Executive conference room in which Senior Managers often worked.

Requirement 5C: Use week-at-a-time scheduling with one-on-one assignments

Mind-Clearing Example—Imagine a Director who is transitioning her theater company while continuing to perform the old play. Imagine the Director continuing to use a detailed daily schedule of performances for the old play (specific days and times for each performance, days when there will be cast substitutions, etc.). At the same time the director used only a high-level schedule for transition to the new play showing only what months would be devoted to casting, costume fittings, rehearsals, etc.

This step is a simple but often-neglected one. While managers in the organization that is changing need a master schedule to understand what they must do and when they must do it, their workers don't need a detailed schedule of the entire project. The workers do need an overall time frame for making the organizational change. But what they need more is a time schedule that fits their normal work routines. If the current work of their organization is scheduled on a once-a-week basis, change work schedules need to be served up on a once-a-week schedule as well.

If we want workers to continue to do their assigned work in producing products and services while doing change work, we must help them by providing both lead times and scheduling of change work that allows them to make the inevitable adjustments that must be made during times of change. Failure to keep workers informed of needed change work has been the downfall of many organizational changes.

There are few things that hurt worker morale more than having them surprised by elements of the organizational change. The kinds of surprises that we have seen while doing our change management consulting range from the simple, hardly-consequential surprise, to what appear to be life-changing surprises:

- Physical re-locations of the department, including worker desks and on-the-spot moves to another plant—today!

- Disconnecting of phone and/or computer lines without warnings to workers
- Changes in signage renaming departments or work processes
- Impromptu training classes that workers did not know they were to attend or had no time to attend, given their other work responsibilities
- Unexpected arrival of new equipment or tools, or departure of old equipment and tools

The goal is to have each worker see the change work that will be needed from him in time for him to get it done . . . along with the old work that he is still doing on a day-to-day basis. For each week/month of the implementation, we want to show those communication and alteration tasks to be accomplished that week. Keeping well planned and followed schedules for change work in front of workers on a week-to-week or month-to-month basis not only keeps workers informed, but it pays extra benefits as well:

- It says to workers that change work is a regular part of our business along with old product-building, customer-serving work.
- It says to workers that the organization cares enough about them to keep them informed about what is happening in the place where they work.
- It shows orderly progress toward a targeted change-over to new work letting the workers know that the organization is really serious about change.

Mind-Clearing Example—Imagine a Director who schedules all of the actors in his company to show up for a costume fitting at the same time . . . when the seamstress can only handle the one-hour fittings of one actor at a time.

Imagine the Director saying to waiting actors, "Well, I can't do everything for you . . . surely you can handle a little scheduling problem!"

So, where are we? We have developed a vision and communicated that vision across the organization, with particular emphasis on the parts of the organization most affected by the intended change. We have identified all the alterations that will need to be made in the organization's work processes and FET. We have identified the individuals who will be impacted by the change, and we have determined the role alterations that will need to be made by those folks to be in sync with the new work. We have already had an important one-on-one conversation with each affected employee to get him under agreement to perform the new way of doing business after change-over, to continue old work until change over, and to perform the needed change work to get ready for change over.

Week-at-a-time scheduling with one-on-one assignments is designed to ensure that each worker involved in an organizational change knows exactly what change work she needs to do literally every day until change over. We recommend that managers use one-on-one meetings with each employee affected by an impending change to officially launch the change work that will need to be done by the employee. This one-on-one meeting reaffirms that we have the worker under agreement to do the change work. Managers might drop in on workers every week to say things like this, "Charlie, remember that we have system training Thursday afternoon, OK?"

After the one-on-one conversation about change work, workers may continue to address change work as needed with the assistance of a weekly schedule. But more one-on-one conversations will need to be held during scheduled change work to ensure that the worker has the support, direction, and resources necessary to get the change work done along with his old work.

We have found that change engineering work gets kicked off much better with much greater likelihood of results when there has been a face-to-face conversation between manager and employee about upcoming events such as training classes, office moves, familiarization sessions on new equipment, etc. Merely posting a change schedule on a bulletin board near affected workers will not get them launched on the path to change.

We must keep the workers' situation in clear perspective to ensure that we can support this critical step in organizational change. It is important to keep in mind that workers in the midst of change are like the theater company members who are called on to perform the old play every evening while they spend parts of the day-time hours getting ready for the new play.

During this critical phase of completing change work, workers still have responsibility for completing old work during the time periods when they will also be attending training classes, executing office moves, and so on. It falls to the manager of those workers to provide the support needed to be able to accomplish two critical things at once. Managers can arrange to have other workers cover for those workers who are in training classes, arrange for temporary employees to do some of the old work—or the change work for that matter—such as executing parts of office moves.

This one-on-one meeting step calls for some big shifts in what many managers do on a daily basis. It is quite common for managers in a smoothly running organization doing old work to have very infrequent contact with workers. After all, everybody knows what to do and how to do it and everybody is going about business as usual. When it is time for change work to get done in an orderly and systematic way, it is critical that the manager change the frequency of contact with workers. Bottom line, we want to ensure that each individual who has a task to do in implementation of a change has a clear assignment and responsibility for doing that work and has the day-by-day support of her supervisor in getting that work done.

> **PPI Example 5C: Use week-at-a-time scheduling with one-on-one assignments**
>
> *During the problem solving phases of change projects, one-on-one scheduling was handled by the project manager. When the projects reached the implementation stage, the line managers in whose department the changes were to be made were responsible for the one-on-one scheduling of change work for his work force.*

OPM NOTE 5C

As one might imagine, PPI's disciplined use of RTB/CTB carried over into the change projects. Each change projects was treated as "very serious business," not as a "day in the park". Projects were treated seriously, and they achieved serious business results.

Requirement 5D: Regularly check transition progress and re-schedule as needed

Mind-Clearing Example—Imagine a Director who sets a schedule for the transition to the new play but who never checks the schedule. When asked by the Producer how the transition is going, the Director says, "Oh, fine, I guess. Didn't I give you a schedule a couple of months ago when we started the transition?"

"Never a horse that ain't been rode, never a cowboy who ain't been thrown." And never a change effort that goes just the way it is planned. Change leaders can count on many things about the organizational change to go differently than planned. This fact does not in any way lessen the need for good planning and scheduling. They are the best tools for dealing with the inevitable interruptions, diversions, and obstacles that appear almost by magic in the path of every organizational change.

Organizations that have mastered change expect the unexpected, continually monitor for implications for the change initiative, and aggressively re-schedule change work to keep the overall change initiative on track. Successful organizations clearly and quickly re-communicate modified schedules.

Expect the unexpected

The change leader can count on several of the following situations to occur on his watch:

- Shifts in demand for the organization's goods and services
- Turnover of key members of the organization

- Problems with key customers (they change a big order, they cancel a big order, they stop making referrals, and so on)
- Competitive challenges (introduction of competitive products, decreases in competitor prices)
- Interruption of critical supplies to the organization
- Introduction of new regulations or organizational policies.

In addition to the situations above, the change leader can expect there to be surprises in the change work itself:

- Equipment installation takes longer and costs more than planned
- Equipment that gets installed but doesn't work the way it was intended
- Training sessions that do not enable employees to achieve the needed level of proficiency
- Workers who change their minds about staying in their current position and moving to the new way of doing business
- Communication glitches that foster confusion and misunderstanding
- Change leaders such as key task force members, project schedulers, etc. who leave the organization or transfer to a part of the organization that is not involved in the change, and so on . . .

When these inevitable situations occur, the change leader must face two realities: first, these situations must be satisfactorily handled, and, second, the organizational change initiative must continue movement toward the change . . . on target, on time, and on schedule. There are, of course, some situations that occur that might cause the change initiative to be cancelled, but those are usually rare.

Monitor Run-the-Business to find implications for change work

Imagine a director who was so engrossed in preparation for his company's new play that he did not notice major problems in the night-to-night performance of the old play. Closer to reality for most of us, image the change leader who is so intent on making the organizational change on target, on time, and on budget that she does not see what is happening to the current work of the organization. The change leader must be focused both on the running of today's business (because that's what pays the current bills for the organization!) and the changing of the organization (because that's what will pay the bills in the future!).

As each day goes by, the change leader must identify those situations which might impact his change effort and determine the potential implications of those situations. The two major kinds of implications that we want to watch for are as follows:

- **Obstacles to change work:** Situations that will require an organizational response that will in some way interrupt the important actions on the master schedule and/or the change budget. An example might be a crisis eruption with an important customer that requires most of the personnel in a department to drop everything and rescue the situation even though they were scheduled for training on new work processes.

- **Issues with the design of the change:** Issues here are of two kinds. First, as the change begins to unfold, flaws may be found in the design of the vision itself. It may be that the potential value of the vision may not prove to be as great as once envisioned. In that case, the vision may need to be altered, requiring modifications in the change work to be done. Second, the business environment outside the organization might change, impacting the potential effectiveness of the vision. Once again, the vision may require modification.

Re-schedule to keep momentum

The two main drivers to the re-scheduling process are (1) the interruptions and obstacles that we have just discussed and (2) what the organization is learning during the change process. As the change work unfolds in the organization, some parts of the change are likely to go better than expected. For example, we could learn that training a department in the new work processes takes only half as long as expected. Or we might learn that the installation of FET costs less and/or occurred faster than originally planned. Any of the lessons learned during the change might be used to produce a re-schedule that is more effective and/or more efficient. Managers who have mastered change expect to see these learnings and are prepared to take advantage of them quickly in the re-schedule and re-budget process.

There are two approaches to the re-schedule process that we have learned to use simultaneously.

- **Schedule extension approach:** The first approach is to treat all schedule changes as alterations to the last and most current schedule. In this first approach, we are keeping the logic and sequence of the very first scheduling process in play as we identify needed schedule alterations called for by interruptions and obstacles.

- **Zero-based scheduling approach:** The second approach is like the familiar zero-based budgeting concept and calls for us to periodically re-think the overall logic and rationale of the entire master schedule. We stimulate this kind of thinking with questions like the following: If we were setting our master schedule today for the first time, what general order and logic would we use? Given what we know today about the organizational situation, how would we lay out the change work needed before change over?

The use of both these mindsets or approaches produces the best overall way to look at re-scheduling. The most difficult change management environment our firm has ever worked in required re-thinking the change work schedule every Monday morning to take into account unfolding business events of the previous week. Not every change situation will be as complex as this engagement, but regularly re-thinking the schedule has proven to be a critical skill for our consultants.

Yes, most re-scheduling efforts will be driven by the simple need to go around logistical obstacles. But sometimes we will find the clear need to alter the logic or sequence in the change schedule. The change leader must always keep in mind that he is doing two things at once: supporting the organization as it continues to do old work of getting out its products and services to today's customers, while keeping change momentum in place for an organizational change that is on target, on time, and on budget.

Quickly re-communicate new schedules

When re-schedules are necessary, and they will be necessary; it is important to quickly and clearly communicate the new schedules to those organization members who need them. If you have assigned qualified project managers to assist in change leadership, they will be versed in requirements of critical path scheduling and re-scheduling. They will have established guidelines for keeping track of schedules to ensure that the organization always has the current schedule. Obviously in big complicated change projects with many moving parts, just keeping track of who has what schedule can become a big job. Clearly the current movement toward web-based project management and scheduling can be a major tool for ensuring both currency and availability of good schedules.

Unfortunately, strong project management will never be enough. Strong and diligent executive leadership must back the project managers and in some case, actually communicate any re-directs or re-schedules. Regardless of how well organized the change project, strong committed leadership with the right level of authority will be required every time.

PPI Example 5D: Regularly check progress and reschedule

We discussed in an earlier PPI example the performance improvement and change projects that were led by the PPI CEO and project teams. The Management Council and the Business Strategy Council were like the Steering Committees shown on the organization charts earlier in this chapter. The Management council had regular monthly meetings during which each project manager briefed project progress, issues, and next steps. Project issues were discussed and problem solved in real-time in the meeting, and the meeting provided the information each project manager needed to revise his project master schedule as needed.

> Project managers reported directly to the Management Council but since the CEO was a member of the council, there was a direct connection between projects and the boss. When the CEO was absent from the council meeting, the Director of Quality represented him in the meetings.

OPM NOTE 5D

> The CEO and the Director of Quality met several times per week to cover both normal business and to talk about the status of the organizational change. They discussed what was working and not working in the initiatives for Perfect Service and in changing change.

Requirement 5E: Confirm, stabilize and celebrate the completed change

> *Mind-Clearing Example—Imagine a Director who hears by the grapevine that transition work has been done . . . but who never goes or sends anyone to check to make sure. Imagine the director at a Pre-opening Night Party toasting to the company, "If it's not done by now, we'll find out after the curtain goes up tomorrow night!"*

Old time managers who have "been there and done that" tell us to "expect what you inspect." Now I know that such trite phrases have lost much of their popularity in an era of participative management and flat organizations, but show me a theater Director who will move confidently to opening night without multiple dress rehearsals. Show me a Producer who feels confident to face investors with the words of the Director, "Aw, we don't need full dress rehearsals; it just wastes valuable time and puts wear and tear on the set and costumes!"

This confirmation step is designed to test the organization's final readiness to execute the change-over to new work. It is also about finding those last remaining trouble spots that must be ironed out before the organizational change can be made . . . on target, on time, and on budget. This step is one more opportunity to reinforce the change that is about to happen for the company's and employees' betterment.

Make sure that alterations have really been made

The truth of the matter in change management is that the organization is not ready for change until it is ready, and a change-over should not start without confirming that needed alterations in work processes, FET, and employee agreements have been completed. So the message here is simple: double check to make sure! But the change leader's goal in this confirmation step should be to come across as a leader, not just an inspector.

The best way to check and confirm that change work has been done is as follows:

- **Work processes:** Look at process diagrams for the new work; look for new procedures; see if you can find the old procedure manuals that are marked for destruction after change-over date, etc.

- **Facilities, Equipment, Technology (FET):** Look at newly-installed FET; view equipment test results; look for new operating guidelines; and view the plans for taking old equipment out of play after change over, etc.

- **Performance management:** Interview employees; ask them to tell you about the new roles they will be performing; ask them to walk through the new work processes they will be performing; check their understanding of the change-over date.

Completion of these confirmation steps will provide some confirmations of change and some confirmations of problems. Once problems are identified, then the master schedule must be modified to reflect those actions that will be needed to complete Change Work.

Confirming readiness for change-over also includes checking for currency. For some of the mechanical properties of organizations, the saying "Once changed, always changed" just does not apply. For example, training records might reflect that training has been completed;

but employees may not be "current." Training workers too far in advance of the change-over will usually be wasted . . . because none of us retains new knowledge or skill without putting it to use.

Celebrate successful completion of change work

So why do theater folks hold those "preview" performances, followed by cocktails for the theater company and selected members of the specially-invited audience? Preview performances accomplish a number of things that the change leader also needs to accomplish:

- **Final check on readiness:** Preview performances serve as additional dress rehearsals used to hone the theater company's readiness

- **Ending of change work:** Preview performances are confirmation with the cast that preparation is ending and the new play is about to open, symbolically moving to the new way of doing business

- **Thanks for change work:** Preview performances show appreciation for the hard work of preparation—"We recognize and value your hard work to change to the new way of doing business

- **Commitment:** And preview performances are the last confirmation of full commitment of each and every member of the company to the new play.

Organizations cannot hold a preview performance as easily as a theater company . . . but they can do something to get many of the effects of one. We recommend to our change management clients that they hold a celebration near the time of the change-over to symbolically confirm readiness and commitment. Such a celebration also says thank you to workers who have been getting ready for the change. We want the celebration to add energy, enthusiasm, and momentum to the individuals, teams, and units involved in the implementation of change.

OPM NOTE 5E

At the end of his first year, the CEO judged the company's progress to be good . . . but did not rest on any laurels. He and his Executive Team dug in and set even more challenging RTB/CTB goals. He was particularly pleased with the way the Run-the-Business and Change-the-Business Management Systems had worked. The CEO insisted that PPI stay with the dual Management System model and continue to refine it . . . and they did . . . for the next decade.

And in conclusion . . .

CEO: "After ten years of profitable growth, PPI's parent company decided that commodity plastics would not be part of its strategic focus for the future. As a result of the performance we had exhibited at PPI, our owners were able to profitably merge our operation with an industry giant's chemical group.

> *"The management model that allowed us to focus on both Run-the-Business and Change-the-Business was the key to our success . . . and kept us from becoming bogged down in the details of day-to-day operations!"*
>
> *Within twelve months of the merger/purchase, the company's RTB/CTB method fell into disuse because the new parent company had its own method of dealing with organizational change!*

In today's turbulent world, trying to lead an organizational change without Organizational Project Management may be an act of futility and frustration for all involved. The many moving parts of change must be managed in a very disciplined fashion or disorder will result. A major theme of this book has been to treat change work as a project . . . using a formal project manager with the authority and resources needed to get change work done. When project management is used in conjunction with the change formula we have presented in this book, an organizational change can be delivered on target, on time, and on budget.

In order to effectively implement OPM, we must use the type of approach we would like to see once OPM has become an integral component of our organization. This is often called "eating your own dog food." We must use the methods, techniques, and tools to put in place OPM that we want to see in place once the OPM implementation has been completed. Effective project management is the key.

Conclusion:
The New Paradigm at Work

Chapter Nine

The New Paradigm at Work

Mind-Clearing Example—Imagine a Director and his Producer partner who stay focused on the current play and never seem concerned about the next play. They frequently wait until investors complain about their declining profits from the current play before even thinking about the next play. Their motto is to let "a lack of cash flow" motivate them to begin planning for the next production.

It is an inescapable fact that today's companies must Run-the-Business and, at the same time, Change-the-Business. While today's companies are usually highly skilled in Running-the-Business, the management of most companies is "competence-challenged" in Changing-the-Business. To correct this inconvenient and uncomfortable truth, businesses need to immediately transition to the New Paradigm for doing business. It is both critical and urgent for companies to begin to operate with two complementary Management Systems as shown in Figure 9.1.

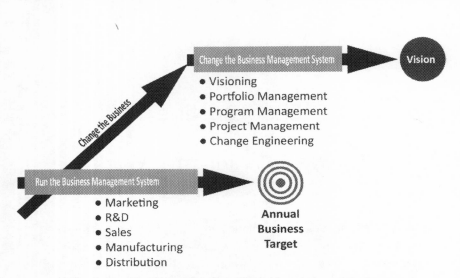

Figure 9.1: The New Paradigm: Two Management Systems

The emerging discipline of Change-the-Business/Organizational Project Management (CTB/OPM) is gaining in popularity as it develops into a more mature discipline and as that discipline produces positive business results for companies that realize the need for a more orderly and effective change management process (Figure 9.1). In this book we have shown OPM with five key disciplines that must be both integrated and tuned to work together at the level of formality needed to meet organizational goals.

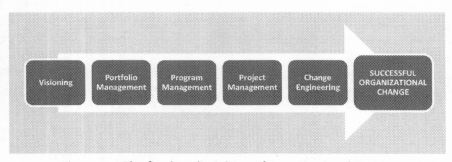

Figure 9.2: The five key disciplines of Organizational Project Management

OPM, with its five different disciplines, is not a piece of cake to implement in a company that is Running-the-Business at full speed in order to meet the current year's profit targets. We have described in this book, however, an effective and efficient method of making the organizational changes needed to put OPM or any other organizational change into day-to-day operation.

An organizational change is successful if it helps the organization move to a higher level of performance. We change organizations in order to make the future better for all stakeholders: customers, investors, and employees. Why go through all the effort of making an organizational change if it is not going to help the organization thrive?

For the most part, organizations today are attempting to make important changes happen without a discipline like OPM. Almost 70% of change initiatives fail to meet management expectations for two primary reasons:

- Failing to break organizational change into right sized programs and projects that can be managed successfully.
- Using what have proven to be invalid methodologies for organizational change.

In this book, we have attempted to turn both reasons for failure to "right actions" for successful organizational change.

1. **Right Action: Translating an organizational change initiative into right-sized projects**. Successful organizational change depends upon breaking change initiatives into a set of smaller projects, each of which must be managed to completion with Program and Program Management and Change Engineering.

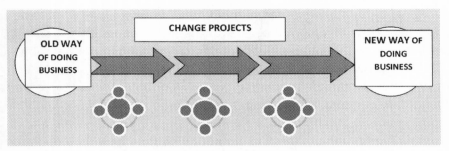

Figure 9.3: Multiple change projects for successful
organizational change

2. **Right Action: Using a valid change formula:** Successful change requires the use a proven formula for making organizational changes happen . . . on target, on time, and on budget. Failure to use the formula will result in project failures which will doom the entire change initiative.

Successful organizational change depends on precise use of the change formula:

a. Communicating an exciting vision of a better way of doing business
b. Creatively altering work processes that enable the better way
c. Incorporating robust and powerful FET to enable altered work processes, and
d. Re-structuring challenging and engaging roles for employees in the new way of doing business.

Successful change also depends on the use of disciplined project management that ensures that all the organization's moving parts are prepared and positioned properly for a new and better way of doing business.

References and Readings

1. *Change Is the Rule: Practical Actions for Change . . . On Target, On Time, and On Budget,* Winford E. Dutch Holland, Chicago: Dearborn Press (2000).
2. *Organizational Project Management Maturity Model,* (Opm3r) Knowledge Foundation, Project Management Institute (2008).
3. *How Managers can Thrive in Waves of Change,* Dutch Holland, PhD, Bloomington: Xlibris (2012).
4. *The Social Psychology of Organizations,* Daniel Katz and Robert L. Kahn, Wiley (1978).
5. *Organizations in Action: Social Science Bases of Administrative Theory,* James D. Thompson, Mayer N. Zald and W. Richard Scott, Transactions Publishers (2003).
6. *Competitive Strategy: Techniques for Analyzing Industries and Competitors,* Michael E. Porter, Free Press (1998)
7. *Project Management: Strategic Design and Implementation,* David I. Cleland and Lewis R. Ireland: New York: McGraw-Hill (2002).
8. *The Management of Innovation,* Tom Burns and G. M. Stalker, Oxford University Press (1994)
9. *Red Zone Management: Project Management for the Executive Suite,* Winford E Dutch Holland, Chicago: Dearborn Press (2001 and 2004).
10. *A Guide to the Project Management Body of Knowledge: PMBOK(R) Guide,* Project Management Institute (Jan 1, 2013)

Appendix A

Task List for Successful Organizational Change

Appendix A

Work Breakdown Elements
for Successful Organizational Change

1. Engineering and Communicating the Vision of OPM
   a. Construct the detailed vision for organizational change
   b. Construct the partner to the vision: the case for change
   c. Ensure management understanding and expectation
   d. Communicate the vision the right way to the entire organization
   e. Ensure employee translation of the vision

2. Engineering and Altering processes and procedures for OPM
   a. Identify process alterations needed for a transition
   b. Alter and test processes critical for a transition
   c. Alter process measures, goals, and objectives to match the direction of the transition
   d. Alter and test work procedures for altered processes
   e. Eliminate old measures, goals, objectives and procedures

3. Engineering Altering the facilities/equipment/tools (the FET) for OPM
   a. Identify the FET alterations needed for each transition
   b. Alter and test all the FET needed in each transition
   c. Alter and test each and every FET control
   d. Alter or create written guidelines for all involved FET
   e. Eliminate old FET and operating guidelines

4. Engineering Altering the performance management system for OPM
   a. Identify and alter individual roles and goals needed for transition

b. Complete one-on-one contracting for every person affected by the transition
c. Train all employees in the roles they will play after the transition
d. Identify and alter the system for monitoring performance
e. Alter and communicate compensation payoffs for work after the transition

5. Engineering Project management for the OPM Initiative
   a. Set and communicate the master schedule for transition work
   b. Use week-at-a-time transition or implementation scheduling
   c. Make one-on-one transition assignments
   d. Regularly check transition progress and reschedule
   e. Confirm and celebrate the completed transition

Appendix B

Detailed Steps and Scripts for Selected Chapters

Appendix of Detailed Steps and Scripts for
Chapter Four
Communicate the Vision

A good way to detail a vision is to simply put a vision team in a room and ask them to write on wall charts answers to the following sets of questions:

- ***Organization Members:*** *Who will be working or behaving in new ways after the desired change is put into effect? How will they be acting that is different than they act today? What will be the accepted way they will be doing things around here? Where will they be located in the organization? Who will they be relating to or working with that is different than today? How will that interaction look? How will those workers be incentivized?*

- ***Work Processes:*** *What work processes or steps for getting work done will be different than the steps that are being used now? What parts of the organization will be doing things differently after the change? What will they be doing for customers that they are doing today?*

- ***FET:*** *What tools will people be using in work processes? What buildings in what location will they be in? What kind of desktop will they have? What software will the people be using in different parts of the organization? What will this software be doing for them? What will they be doing "on the screen" vs. "off the screen?"*

Once the vision team has sketched answers to the questions, the team (or an appointed small drafting committee) can combine the team's answers into a form that will make sense for the situation . . . either a short story format or a highly-detailed bullet point slide presentation.

Test the vision for organizational change

We think a good way to do the test of the vision is to get a cross-sectional group of a dozen employees together in a briefing room and brief them on the vision. Let them read the vision if it is in text form. Then ask them to answer the following questions (putting the folks into three teams of four helps the responses):

1. What did you hear as the Vision for this organization's future?
2. Can you see how this Vision will work to win with customers, investors, and employees?
3. What parts of the Vision need more detail for the sake of clarity?
4. Can you see the organization being successful in implementing this Vision?
5. Do you think the organization can get the resources it needs to achieve this Vision?
6. What about the Vision will be attractive, engaging, and challenging to the organization and its workers?
7. Is this a Vision that you could explain to others in the organization? What parts of the Vision would be tough to explain?

When you look at the responses to questions like these, you will know whether you have stated your Vision in a way the organization can understand. If answers from the test employees show that they understand the Vision, find it doable and compelling, you may have a vision that will serve you well in the change process. If not, clarify or add more detail to the vision. But whatever you do, don't start an organizational change initiative without a clear and understandable vision for the future.

Conducting management work-through sessions

Given these stated conditions, we have found the following structure to be useful in Management Work Though Sessions:

1. The organization's leader(s) start the management meeting with an introduction that explains the purpose of the session.

a.   Our purpose today is to talk through an organizational change that we will be making to ensure the prosperity/survival of our company

b.   My expectation is that you will involve yourself in the session to fully understand the change that all of us, the company's management team, will be responsible for implementing.

2.   The leader follows with a description of the impending change (e.g., the vision . . . including the organizational structure) and the rationale for the change.

3.   The leader breaks the audience of managers into small teams of four to five to discuss and report on the following questions:

a.   What did you hear as the most important part of the vision?

b.   What did you hear as the most important business reason for the organizational change?

c.   What are the advantages to the company of the impending change?

d.   What are the disadvantages of remaining the way we are?

e.   What are the disadvantages of the impending change?

f.   What are the biggest obstacles to fully implement the change?

g.   What are your ideas about the best ways to go about the implementation of such a change?

4.   The leader moves from team to team, making herself available for questions and clarifications as the teams work through the questions.

5.   The leader calls for the teams to present their answers to the questions and arranges for those answers to be recorded for later use.

a.   The leader's goal during this step is to hear the audience working through the understanding and assimilating of information about the impending change.

b.   The leader's challenge will be to hear these answers as part of a communication process and not direct criticism of the leader's choice of a direction for impending change.

6. The leader now shifts emphasis and asks each individual manager to consider the following questions for his/her organization:

    a. What will be the ramifications of the change for your part of the organization?
    b. In presenting the impending change to your organization (unit, department, section, etc.), what will be the most critical part of the case for change?

7. The leader might ask for volunteers (three or four managers) to share their answers with the audience.

8. The leader wraps up the discussion by asking the audience of managers to respond as one large team—because that is what they are—to the following questions:

    a. On a one to seven scale, how clear are we on the vision of the impending change?
    b. On a one to seven scale, how clear are we on the case for the change?

9. The leader records the number of responses in each category, one to seven (with seven meaning "very clear") and responds to the results. A normal audience that hears and understands an impending change will have a normal distribution of scores around the "five to six" points on the seven-point scale. If there are scores in the three to four range, the leader can ask the general audience (without identifying the managers whose scores were low) how she might further clarify the vision and case for organizational change.

10. The leader closes the sessions with the following announcements:

    a. We appreciate your input in developing clarity around the change statements
    b. We will get back together again to discuss and finalize our action plans for implementing the impending change
    c. Before that meeting, I (or your boss) will visit with each of you one-on-one to ensure we are in sync about the change.

Use proven communication principles

There are four principles that we believe are required for effective communication about impending organizational change.

1. **Two-way communication**—that allows organization members to ask questions and give feedback about the change—is required for a high comprehension level. We all need to interact in the communication process if we are to really "get" a message that is being communicated.

2. **Communication Bases** should be considered when planning and executing communication. In short, some adults understand new messages better if they see them in black and white; other understand better if they hear them; others need to experience the message by handling physical models or imagining themselves in the described situation. Since organizations are made up of all three communication types, leaders must ensure that their communication plan provides devices that cover all three bases.

3. **Repetition** is required for any of us to get organization messages. While the number of needed repetitions has been quoted in the literature from three to four all the way to seven or more, our position is simple. Plan to communicate to every single person in the organization significantly more times than once to ensure the message about impending change is delivered.

4. **Rich, face-to-face communication** is required for organization members to communicate at maximum levels of effectiveness on critically-important subjects. Messages about impending organizational change must be delivered face-to-face or organization members will not have their communication needs at all met. Put the details in a follow-up letter that comes later . . . but put the essential messages about impending change in play in a face-to-face environment.

Face-to-face communication can be a real problem in today's world of companies that are dispersed over the country or the globe. Employees in dispersed locations have to hear about change in face-to-face meetings with their local bosses. And the local bosses need to hear it first from their boss back at headquarters. That usually means travel—there is no way around it, although Skype and Go-to-Meeting are pretty handy.

Agree to and use communication standards

All managers involved in the communication of change must be in sync with how they are going to communicate to the organization. We have found it useful to get the mangers to agree on standards for communication that provides basic guidelines for the communication process.

1. Communication of the change will be done from a comprehensive, coordinated plan.
2. All change messages will be developed and delivered ensuring that:

   a. There is a redundancy of message delivery (i.e., each employee receives the message multiple times)
   b. The message will be delivered through a variety of channels (verbal, written, face-to-face meetings, newsletters, training programs)

3. All messages will be tested for understandability before delivery
4. We will ensure that our management actions match the words in our message

Imagine how well communication might work in an organization if all its managers agreed to and used such communication standards. One of the primary responsibilities of any manager is to communicate important messages about the running of the organization. When managers begin to take such responsibility seriously, organization change will get much easier than it is today in many organizations who treat communication as "just more of that soft stuff!"

We have found the following structure useful for the sessions between managers and their teams of employees.

1. The manager starts the meeting with an introduction that explains the purpose of the session.

    a. Our purpose today is to talk through an organizational change that we will be making to ensure the prosperity/survival of our company

    b. The goal of this session is to help you understand the impending change, what it will mean to you and your job, and to get your initial sign up for the change. We also want your suggestions about how to make the change.

2. The manager follows with a description of the impending change, (the VISION and the Case for the Change.

3. The manager breaks the audience of employees into small teams of three to four to discuss and report on the following questions:

    a. What did you hear as the most important part of the VISION?

    b. What did you hear as the most important business reason for the organizational change?

    c. What do you see as the changes we will need to make in our jobs in this department?

    d. What are your ideas about the best ways to implement such a change in your work area?

4. The manager walks among the groups making herself available for questions and clarifications as the teams work through the questions.

5. The manager calls for the teams to present their answers to the questions and arranges for those answers to be recorded for later use.

6. The manager now shifts emphasis and asks each individual to consider the following questions for his/her job:

   a. What will be the ramifications of the change for your job?
   b. What kinds of things will you need to change in your specific job?

7. The manager might ask for three or four volunteers to share their answers with the audience.

8. The manager wraps up the discussion by asking the employees to respond as one large team to the following questions:

   a. On a one to seven scale, how clear are we on the general direction of the impending change?
   b. On a one to seven scale, how clear are we on the Case for the Change?

9. The manager records the number of responses in each category, one to seven (with seven meaning "very clear") and responds to the results. A normal audience that hears and understands an impending change will have a normal distribution of scores around the four to six points on the seven-point scale. If there are scores in the two to three range, the leader can ask the general audience (without identifying the workers whose score were low) how she can further clarify the Vision and Case for Organizational Change.

10. The manager closes the Session with the following announcements:

    a. We will get back together again to discuss and finalize our Action Plans for Implementing the impending change
    b. Before that meeting, I will visit with each of you one-on-one to ensure we are in sync about the change.

Appendix of Detailed Steps and Scripts for
Chapter Five
Alter Work Processes and Procedures

Use a Team to Identify the Alterations Needed in Work Processes

We have found that one of the easier ways to identify work process impacts is to convene a team of employees who know the organization very well and have them go through either the company work process inventory or the generic inventory and look for connections between those processes and the VISION. The exercise that we use is a purely mechanical one. We give the team the following instructions:

1. Spend fifteen minutes getting as clear as you can on the VISION

2. Working from the actual or generic inventory list, answer the following questions for each work process in your organization:

    a. Can we reach our VISION if the steps in this work process stay exactly like they are now?
    b. If "No," what steps must be altered to allow us to enact the VISION?
    c. For each step that needs to be altered, what should be the desired result of that alteration?

3. Compile the results of your team's deliberations into the following categories:

    a. Work processes that do not need alteration
    b. Work processes that do need alteration

    c.   *Steps in each work process that need alteration and needed result of that alteration*

4. *Label your team's compiled results as "Process Alterations Needed to Reach the VISION" and prepare to give team results during the Action Planning Requirement.*

Use a Team to Map and Test Work Processes

We have found that a team of knowledgeable employees can map work processes to show needed alterations. After forming the Alteration Team, we give the following instructions:

1. *Review the previously compiled "Process Alterations Needed to Reach the Vision"*
2. *For each Process that has been identified as needing alteration, re-draw the process work steps from beginning to end, describing those steps as necessary to achieve the desired result*
3. *Mentally test each altered work process for effectiveness and efficiency (will this step work? Will it contribute to the desired result?)*
4. *Identify the kind of tools (plant, equipment, hand tools, machine tools, hardware, software) that would be needed by workers to perform the altered processes (more will be said about FET in Chapter Six)*
5. *Identify the staffing/training requirements for the altered work processes (number of workers, kind of workers, needed skills)*
6. *Identify the kind of real-life test that would be needed to insure the altered work processes will work*
7. *NOTE WORK PROCESS AND FET EVALUATION WOULD BE PERFORMED AT THE SAME TIME*

After this working session, the most important thing the Alteration Team has to get done is to arrange and conduct the test of altered processes. Of course the results of the test may lead to a confirmation or revision of the maps of the altered processes.

Alter Process Measures, Goals and Objectives
to Match the Direction of Change

Use a Team to Identify Needed Alterations in Measures, Goals, and Objectives. We have used the same Work Process Alteration Teams to modify measures, goals, and objectives. We use the following instructions to get the Teams focused on the task at hand:

1. Re-examine the "Process Alterations Needed to Reach the Vision" completed in an earlier step

2. Review those processes where step alterations are not needed, and answer the following questions:

   a. Will we be able to reach the desired Vision if all measures, goals, and objects remain unchanged?
   b. If "No," what changes must be made in measures, goals, or objectives for each work process and sub-process?

3. Review those processes where step alterations are needed and answer the following question:

   a. What measures, goals or objectives must be set for each altered work process or sub-process for the Vision to be realized?

4. Label your team's compiled results as "Process Performance Measures, Goals, Objectives Needed to Reach the Vision" and prepare to give team results in the Action Planning Phase that comes later.

Appendix of Detailed Steps and Scripts for
Chapter Six
Alter Facilities, Equipment, and Technology (FET)

One of the easier ways to identify FET alterations is to convene a team made up of members of those professions who know how both the organization's current FET and new FET work and employees who will use the new FET and/or employees who will work in the physical location that will be the new FET's home. We give the team the following instructions:

1. Study the Vision, and understand what is being done and why.
2. Study the work processes, plans, and specifications that make up the new FET, and identify alterations needed in present FET
3. Find additional needed alterations in existing FET with a systems analysis of current FET. Conduct walk-through inspections of both the physical and cyber work areas that will receive the new FET. Identify direct connections that will need to be made between new and existing FET. Direct connections include physical changes, equipment, staff resources, training etc. In addition, look for changes in the indirect connections or impacts that may require alterations in existing FET or operation (upstream and downstream department impact, communication systems, supplies, etc.).
4. Discover additional alterations that were not visible on the walk through inspection.
5. Compile the results of the team's deliberations into the following categories:

- FET that does need alteration
- The kind and nature of alteration needed for each piece of FET

6. Label your team's compiled results as "FET Alterations Needed to Reach the Vision." Prepare to give team results during action planning.

Approach Two: The process Inventory approach to Identify needed FET alterations

We have found that one of the easier ways to identify FET alterations is to convene a team that has three different perspectives: employees intimately involved in identifying needed work process alterations, technical folks who know the organization's current and new FET and employees who would be the likely users of the new or altered FET after transition to the new way of doing business. We give the team the following instructions:

1. Study the Vision and understand what is being done and why.
2. Study the alterations that will be made in the work processes in order to enact (the compiled report from the Process Alteration team is required here).
3. Visualize the FET that would be needed to support the work processes that would be altered to enact the Vision of Change. Identify both FET that will need to be acquired and existing FET that would need to be altered.
4. Obtain copies of plans, processes, and specifications for the new FET and identify alterations needed in present FET.
5. Find additional needed alterations in existing FET by conducting a walk through inspection of the work area that will receive the new FET. Identify direct and indirect connections that will need to be made between new and existing FET.
6. Conduct a second walk through along work process lines. Follow the path of the organization's service from start to end, and identify the kind of FET that will be needed.
7. Study the plans and specifications for the existing FET that will need to be modified to discover additional alterations that were not visible on the walk through inspection:
8. Compile the results of your team's deliberations into the following categories:

    a. the kind and nature of alteration needed for each piece of FET
    b. FET that does not need alteration

9. Label your team's compiled results as "FET Alterations Needed to Reach the Vision" and prepare to give team results during action planning.

A Very Special Case: The Alteration of Software

Regardless of the reason for the problem, the change leader must get in control of the requirement definition situation to ensure that the software alterations that are identified accurately reflect the FET changes needed to reach the Vision. We have found the following steps to be useful for the change leader when she works with IT professionals in requirements definition:

1. Meet with the IT professional and explain the organizational change that is driving the need for software alteration
2. Go over in as much detail as you can the new way of doing business.
3. Go over in detail the work process alterations that are being made to accommodate the organizational change. Go over the entire work process change, not just the parts to be automated.
4. Work with the IT professionals to identify who will be interviewed and asked questions to identify user requirements for the software alteration (it clearly helps to have members of the Process Alteration team be a part of the population to be interviewed).
5. Have the IT professional walk through his requirements definition approach with you (this approach will largely consist of questions that he will use in his interviews with the users). Identify the questions in the approach that best address the FET alteration needs as you understand them.
6. Thank the IT professional for helping your change effort . . . then get out of his way while he does his work.
7. When the IT professional completes his requirements definition task, sit down with him and go over his results. Ensure as best you can that the requirements as defined will lead to software alterations that will support the transition to the organization's new way of working. And don't be surprised if what you find leads to additional interviews between you, the interviewees, and the IT professional.

Alter and Test FET Critical for the Change

Use Common Sense Management. For small or simple purchases or installations of FET, it may be OK to use nothing more than the common sense approach . . . but it must be done in a very disciplined way . . . with goals, budgets, and schedules and so on.

Familiar common sense steps of management applied to FET acquisition/ construction:

1. *Get clear on what you are trying to do with the construction project*
2. *Clarify the construction budget and general time schedules if available*
3. *Decide on the equipment to be bought or altered*
4. *Contact vendors who sell or modify that equipment*
5. *Let vendors know what you want, and get a proposal/bid from them*
6. *Evaluate the proposals and choose the vendor(s)*
7. *Lay out the work of the vendor(s) on a time schedule*
8. *Calculate the total dollars likely to be involved*
9. *Secure management approval of the budget and schedule*
10. *Get vendors under contract and started on the job*
11. *Monitor vendor progress, and manage problems day to day to ensure the successful completion of the project on target, on time, and on budget*
12. *Close out the project with the equipment users, ensure their needs have been met, and ensure the contractors have been paid and have left the premises.*

Appendix of Detailed Steps and Scripts for
Chapter Seven
Alter Performance Management

One of the easier ways to identify needed role and goal alterations and new roles and goals is to convene a team of employees who both know the organization very well and who know the details of the work process alterations that are needed. Have that team go through the two alteration lists (Work Process and FET) to look for contacts with organization members.

We give the team the following instructions:

1. Spend fifteen minutes getting as clear as you can on the vision of the desired new way of doing business
2. Study the Work Process Alteration List
3. Note any FET alterations that go with the alterations in work processes
4. Super-impose the firm's organization charts over the work processes that need to be altered and get a feel for which existing worker roles will be involved with altered processes.
5. Answer the following questions for each work process listed as needing alteration:

   a. Which employee roles touch the work processes to be altered?
   b. How will the roles of those employees who touch the work process need to be altered (i.e., how should their roles be modified to cause them to perform to the needed level in the work processes . . . using the needed FET?)
   c. What goals and objectives must be met by workers in the altered roles?

  d. What totally new roles will be needed in order to get all the work of the altered processes done?

  e. What obsolete roles need to be eliminated or portions of roles realigned?

  f. What goals and objectives must be met by workers in the new roles?

  g. Which roles will need to work together as work teams to get the needed level of performance?

  h. What goals and objectives must be met by each needed work team?

6. Next, as a check to the step you have just completed, go through the organization's existing organization charts/table and the list of all employees. For each position and for each person, answer the following question:

> Will this existing position/person be involved in the altered work processes or the altered FET?

- If "Yes," add that name to the list of roles to be altered along with the nature of the needed role alteration
- If "No," add that name to the list of Roles that will not need to be altered.

7. Compile the results of your team's deliberations and label it as "Role Alterations Needed to Reach the Vision" Organize the list in the following categories:

  a. New roles and goals needed to perform work processes

  b. Existing roles and goals that need to be altered

  c. Direction of each role that needs to be altered

  d. Teams that will need to work together to perform the altered processes along with team goals

  e. Existing roles that will not need to be altered

8. For more complicated or comprehensive organizational changes, the structure of the organization chart might need to be altered to give the best structure to the individual teams and roles. Without going into great detail on organizational design, we want to

identify the way we will organize units—individuals and teams—around the work to perform efficiently to the Vision.

9. *Label your team's compiled results as "New Roles and Existing Role Alterations Needed to Reach the Vision" and prepare to give team results during action planning.*

Conduct the Contracting Session to Get Agreements in place

The contracting meeting is a business meeting, and it needs to have a planned business agenda. We recommend the following outline for the contracting session for an organizational change that will require major alteration in what the employee has been doing (for minor changes, the boss can pick and choose how much of the following outline to use):

1. Statement of the purposes of the contracting meeting

    a. To get the employee on board for the upcoming organizational change
    b. To get closure on the role we want the employee to play in the future organization

2. Description of the organizational change the company has committed to make

    a. Explanation of the Vision of Change
    b. Explanation of the Case for Change (why make the change at all and why make it now)
    c. Explanation of how the work in the organization will need to be altered to reach the Vision
    d. Explanation of how the FET will need to change
    e. Explanation of roles that will need to change to support the work processes

3. Presentation of the offer to the employee

    a. Description of the role the boss would like the employee to play in the organization for the new way of doing business

b. Description of the level/kinds of goals the employee would have
c. Description of where the employee would fit in the organization
d. Presentation of the salary/title change if any that would go with the altered role and goals
e. Discussion of the offer with questions and answers

4. Ask for acceptance of the offer

   a. We want you to be a part of the organization after the change
   b. Would you be willing to accept our offer?

5. Clarification of next steps

   a. Effective date of the new organization/role
   b. Continuation of present job (Old Work) while organizational change is being prepared
   c. Participation in the Change Work needed to assist in preparing for the change

6. Meeting close with thanks for agreeing to be a part of the change to the new way of doing business.

Appendix C

Three Implementation Phases

The Detailed Three-Phase Roadmap for Implementing OPM

- **Phase I: OPM Awareness & Education**

    a. Explain the high-level commitment for OPM to all managers
    b. Develop awareness of company needs for OPM thinking and implementation
    c. Develop rationale for OPM Implementation
    d. Select framework for Transitioning to OPM, which will include the establishment of a PMO, if not already in place.
    e. Develop OPM implementation champions
    f. Conduct informal OPM implementation assessment
    g. Conduct OPM implementation awareness/education
    h. Develop business case for Phase II: Initial Trial of OPM

- **Phase II: Initial Trial of OPM Concepts & Techniques**

    a. Formally assess OPM Implementation needs
    b. Pinpoint strategic OPM Implementation targets
    c. Develop pilot projects to "learn and do"
    d. Conduct just-in-time OPM training of pilot teams
    e. Make sure pilot results are put into action
    f. Launch other OPM projects in other parts of organization . . . based on need
    g. Develop business case for Phase III: Implementation of OPM thinking and transition to across-the-board implementation

- **Phase III: Integration of OPM thinking and transition to OPM**

  a. Develop and communicate a detailed vision for the company operating with OPM
  b. Develop implementation plans/timeline/measures/goals . . . . Including the target OPM management capability maturity level
  c. Incorporate OPM measures/objectives into performance management system (goals and rewards)
  d. Acquire, formalize, integrate OPM implementation tools
  e. Modify work processes for OPM implementation effectiveness
  f. Take direct actions as needed to raise the OPM capability maturity level to target
  g. Measure OPM implementation results
  h. Identify and maintain an organizational environment supportive of targeted level of OPM implementation

Steps in the Three Phases of OPM Implementation

PHASE ONE: AWARENESS & EDUCATION

- Understand OPM
- Develop rationale /case for change to OPM
- Select framework for Transitioning to OPM
- Develop OPM champions
- Conduct informal OPM assessment
- Conduct OPM awareness/education
- Develop business case for Phase II: Trial / Pilot Projects

Phase I: OPM Awareness & Education

  a. Understand OPM
     i. What is the OPM Landscape (or body of knowledge)?
     ii. How much has been covered?
     iii. What areas are left that must be explored to be able to say "we covered the waterfront" in doing our OPM research?

    iv. What actions must we take to ensure we have done adequate "homework?"

    v. What arrangements do we need to make to ensure that our OPM research stays fresh?

b. Develop awareness of company needs for OPM

    i. What do we know about the company's expressed need for OPM?

    ii. What sorts of things have we heard about that might call for OPM?

    iii. What anecdotes can we point to as evidence that OPM might be of great value?

    iv. Is there data available that could point to the need for OPM?

    v. Who must we talk to in the company to ensure that we really can speak for the organization's need?

    vi. What actions must we take to ensure we have identified the organization's need?

C. Develop initial rationale for OPM Implementation

    i. (This rationale is really a high level business case for the OPM Implementation project. It also is a business case for doing the work and incurring the expense of Phase I)

    ii. What does a business case or rationale need to look like in this company?

    iii. What format has worked well in the past?

    iv. Who needs to be in on the rationale development to have needed credibility?

    v. What process of review will be used to evaluate this rationale?

    vi. What specific actions will we need to take to pull together this rationale?

    vii. What is the basis for the business case for OPM?

        a) What are the company needs that we can point to that are related to OPM?

        b) What are the economic, market, people costs associated with those needs?

       c) What is the proposed approach? How could OPM meet those needs?

       d) What specific actions might the company take to meet the needs with OPM?

       e) What resource budget will be needed to move to the next phase

d. Select Roadmap we will follow to move toward implementation of OPM

   i. Who would need to be in the session where we finalize the roadmap?

   ii. What are the alternative roadmaps for implementation?

   iii. What format should this framework/roadmap take? (i.e., what would be successful in this company's culture?)

   iv. Build the roadmap by reviewing the framework (this document)

   v. How would we need to alter the roadmap to make it suitable for use in this organization? Steps to add? Steps to delete or change?

   vi. What specific actions need to be taken to gain closure on the framework/roadmap?

   vii. How/when will we review the roadmap to add/modify/delete steps?

e. Develop OPM Management champions

   i. Who will likely be the champions for the *business results* from OPM?

   ii. Who will likely be the champions for OPM techniques and tools?

   iii. Who will be the most likely implementers of OPM projects in their units?

   iv. Who are the credible players who must be involved in OPM for it to "stick" in this company?

   v. Who might make a good technical advisory team?

   vi. Who might make a good business steering committee for the OPM project?

   vii. What actions must be taken to get advisor and/or steering groups into place?

   viii. What communication and/or training might be useful for champions and/or groups?

  ix. When would be the best time to put advisor and/or steering groups into place?

 f. Conduct informal OPM assessment
  i. Become familiar with the OPM Maturity Model tool
  ii. Who would be a good informal team to go through the assessment and draw general conclusions about the state of OPM in the company?
  iii. How will we schedule and conduct this event?
  iv. How will we factor our informal findings into the rationale and the plans for awareness and education?
  v. What actions must be taken to complete the informal assessment?

 g. Conduct OPM awareness/education (A&E)

  i. (A&E should be conducted by phase . . . our focus here is for Phase I)
  ii. Communicate with C level executives recognizing that they generally speak "business content" rather than "process-speak" (therefore, whenever possible communicate using business content examples to make progress with process!)
  iii. Communicate using business examples since we are in the "tire business" (refer to the Michelin CIO story in Europe)
  iv. What might an A&E program look like?
  v. Who should be the population for Phase I A&E?
  vi. What should be our objectives for this phase?
   a) (*Examples:* to inform and educate the key decision makers and likely users of Process Management so that they can be helpful in the finding value process)

  vii. What would be the needed content of this A&E?
   a) (*Examples:* background on OPM Project; rationale for an OPM project; the chosen process—Phases I through III; key OPM content material messages; interactive exercise like the informal assessment)

viii. How would we structure the A&E in order to meet our objectives with this population?
ix. What should the communication methods look like for this Phase?
x. Who should be involved as the content presenters/advocates?
xi. How will we do a "trial run" on A&E for Phase I?
xii. How will we assess the effectiveness of Phase I A&E?
xiii. What actions will be required to get A&E scoped, developed, conducted, and evaluated?

h. Develop business case for Phase II

i. (Note: This step may be used as a kind of Phase I summary or it can be placed in Phase II after the formal assessment and after more specific targets have been identified for pilot projects)
ii. Assemble all relevant information and learning from Phase I to be used in the business case
iii. What is our phase-gate decision: would it be to the company's advantage to go forward or not?
iv. Plan to use the business case format that will be seen as acceptable by the organization
v. Set objectives for Phase II
(*Examples:* to learn the value of specific OPM tools and/or acceptance of OPM tools and methods; to identify key factors that must be taken into account in Phase III Integration)
vi. Identify the general kinds, nature, locations and durations of pilots that will be needed to test OPM before moving to a Phase III organization-wide integration
vii. Identify the likely organization impacts and costs for Phase II pilots
viii. Identify the nature and number of OPM service providers that would be needed for adequate support of Phase II pilots
ix. Make the case that shows how Pilot Phase expenses will be warranted before moving to Phase III

Phase II: Initial Trial of OPM Enterprise Concepts & Techniques

PHASE TWO: PILOT PROJECTS

- Formally assess OPM needs
- Pinpoint strategic OPM targets
- Develop OPM pilot projects to "learn and do"
- Conduct just-in-time OPM training of pilot teams
- Make sure pilot results are put into action
- Launch other OPM projects ... based on need and visibility
- **Develop business case for Phase III: Organization wide Integration of OPM**

a. Formally assess OPM management needs and current capability/ maturity level

   i. Position the purpose for the assessment

- Communicate the message "this is a baseline for improvement"—not a "grade" where we need to make all "A's" the first time (note, there should not be the "blame game" with the results)

   ii. Conduct independent assessment or formal internal assessment using the OPM Maturity Model framework (as a survey or in a workshop mode)

- How candid are we?
- How much breadth and depth will we achieve?

   iii. Analyze the difference between an Environmental and OPM maturity level (too much difference here prevents advancement)

   iv. Assess the core process areas by level (some processes may be more advanced than others)

   v. Develop an action plan for advancing

   vi. Communicate the assessment results as well as an action plan for achieving the next level

b. Pinpoint and assess strategic work processes and environmental factors and target the needed OPM maturity level

    i. Select a work process that

- Needs improvement
- Provides leverage for improvement to other factors

        o Provides an opportunity to impact environmental factors
        o Provides a visible sign to the rest of the organization that this is worthwhile

- Has support from executive management
- Can be successful in the organization

c. Develop pilot projects around core work process to both "learn and do"

    i. Select pilot projects that the organization will allow learning as well as results
    ii. Develop a process map and matrix with axes of impact and learning opportunities

d. Conduct just-in-time OPM Enterprise training of pilot teams including but not limited to:

    i. OPM principles and techniques
    ii. Process redesign steps
    iii. Team dynamics and teambuilding
    iv. Change management and communication
    v. Metrics

e. Make sure pilot results are put into action
    i. Implement pilot project redesigns and other organizational changes
    ii. Identify and develop action plans for lessons learned
    iii. Implement changes related to lessons learned for other projects and organizational obstacles

    iv. Communicate and recognize
    v.   Communicate and recognize
    vi. Communicate and recognize

f. Launch other OPM projects in other parts of the organization . . . based on need
g. Develop business case for Phase III: Implementation of targeted level

    i.   Assemble all relevant information and learning from Phase II pilot projects to be used in the business case
    ii. What is our phase-gate decision: would it be to the company's advantage to go forward or not?
    iii. Plan to use the business case format that will be seen as acceptable by organization
    iv. Set objectives for Phase III

        o (*Examples:* to increase revenue by x%; to reduce costs by y%; to conduct other organizational changes such as integrate Activity Based Costing across the company)

    v.   Identify the specific changes that will be needed to integrate process and environmental dimensions organization-wide
    vi. Identify the likely organization impacts and costs for Phase III transition
    vii. Identify the nature and number of OPM service providers that would be needed for adequate support of Phase III projects
    viii. Make the case that shows how the Integration expenses will be justified

Phase III: Integration of OPM thinking and transition to the OPM Enterprise

PHASE THREE: WIDE-SPREAD INTEGRATION

- Develop / communicate a detailed OPM vision
- Develop implementation plans / timeline /measures / goals....
- Incorporate OPM measures/objectives into goals and rewards
- Modify work processes for OPM effectiveness
- Acquire, formalize, integrate OPM tools
- Measure OPM results
- **Identify and maintain a supportive environment for the OPM Enterprise**

a. Develop and communicate a detailed vision for the OPM Enterprise
b. Develop implementation plans/timeline/measures/goals . . . . Including the target OPM capability maturity level
c. Incorporate OPM measures/objectives into performance management system (goals and rewards)
    i. Include implementation milestones into goals and rewards initially
    ii. Include implementation results into goals and rewards ultimately

d. Acquire, formalize, integrate OPM tools
    i. Include tools in new employee orientation sessions
    ii. Ensure someone has responsibility and authority to keep tools updated and useful
    iii. Ensure tools are used in the organization when appropriate

e. Modify work processes for OPM effectiveness
    i. Identify and modify enabling processes to increase OPM effectiveness e.g., xxxx

f. Take direct actions as needed to raise the OPM capability maturity level to target
    i. Identify shortfalls
    ii. Understand causes
    iii. Implement changes
    iv. Track results and revise as appropriate

g. Measure OPM results
   i.   Track results
   ii. Identify where results are significantly above/under target and causes
       • actions/process/roles need revision
       • Metrics need revision
       • Organizational obstacles
   iii. Implement changes
   iv. Continue to monitor

h. Identify and maintain an organizational environment supportive of targeted level of OPM
   i.   Define a blueprint of the desired organizational environment
   ii. Define an implementation plan
   iii. Implement (via projects)

CONTACT US!

Put Holland Management Consulting to work for you!

The only way we can be of service is to talk to first. Give us a call, and we can talk about your needs and the needs of your organization . . . and decide how (and "if") HMC might be useful and worth your and your company's investment in time and dollars.

Contact Us

Call us directly at 281.657.3366 . . . our receptionist win ensure that your call will be answered as soon as possible. Email Dutch Holland at *dutch@ hollandmanagementcoaching.com*

Holland Management Consulting
2700 Post Oak Blvd, S 1400
Houston, TX 77056